Unearth the Church

Unearth the Church

Exposing Foundations and Exorcising Selfishness

JOHNMARK CAMENGA

WIPF & STOCK · Eugene, Oregon

UNEARTH THE CHURCH
Exposing Foundations and Exorcising Selfishness

Copyright © 2024 Johnmark Camenga. All rights reserved. Except for brief quotations in critical publications or reviews, no part of this book may be reproduced in any manner without prior written permission from the publisher. Write: Permissions, Wipf and Stock Publishers, 199 W. 8th Ave., Suite 3, Eugene, OR 97401.

Wipf & Stock
An Imprint of Wipf and Stock Publishers
199 W. 8th Ave., Suite 3
Eugene, OR 97401

www.wipfandstock.com

PAPERBACK ISBN: 978-1-6667-8817-4
HARDCOVER ISBN: 978-1-6667-8818-1
EBOOK ISBN: 978-1-6667-8819-8

VERSION NUMBER 030724

Unless otherwise indicated, all Scripture quotations are from the ESV® Bible (The Holy Bible, English Standard Version®), © 2001 by Crossway, a publishing ministry of Good News Publishers. Used by permission. All rights reserved.

Scripture quotations from The Authorized (King James) Version. Rights in the Authorized Version in the United Kingdom are vested in the Crown. Reproduced by permission of the Crown's patentee, Cambridge University Press

Cathy, thank you for knowing me so well—knowing all of my flaws and failings—and still believing in me and encouraging me and loving me. Your questions and perspectives and prayers throughout this process have been far more instrumental than you'll ever know, and this finish line is far sweeter because I'm crossing it with you.
I love you Mary Catherine.

Contents

Introduction | 1
1. Mission Is Revealed by Action | 9
2. Scriptural Mission | 15
3. Modern Mission | 28
4. Outside-In | 35
5. Inside-Out | 48
6. Belief, Action, Fruit | 61
7. The Foundation | 73
8. Conviction | 84
9. Deny Self | 91
10. Covenant | 100
11. Foundation Is Future | 109
12. Next Steps | 114
13. Unearthed Church | 120

Bibliography | 127

Introduction

MANY PEOPLE WHO WERE once active members of churches, faithful attendees of churches, or simply church-adjacent in their day-to-day lives have decided they are done with the church. If you've been in attendance at any church recently, this reality is hard to miss. Pews and parking lots are far emptier than they used to be. Why is this happening?

There have been plenty of articles and books written about the degradation of culture. Podcast after podcast and sermon after sermon decry the crumbling of this moral and the downplaying of that ethic. The church has often been all too eager to latch onto those narratives, claiming that their emptying parking lots and sanctuaries are symptoms of societal illness.

This is the "it's not me, it's you" approach. It is an approach that is rooted in defensiveness and accusation. This approach is just as insulting as it is lazy.

We need to do better.

Instead of taking the easy, blame-game approach, what would happen if the church took a critical glance in the mirror?

When something is unearthed, it is uncovered and exposed. This can be an exciting prospect when it comes to archaeological digs and the discovery of artifacts from ancient civilizations or the skeletal remains of dinosaurs. Seeing those bits of history and speculating what they reveal about people and animals in the past can be an enlightening experience. It is fascinating just how much truth and history is hidden by centuries of dirt and debris.

To unearth the church is similar in some regards. It is a process of digging below the surface to discover what is hiding down there. The discoveries made along the way can be enlightening and fascinating, but they can also be challenging and humbling. In the same way that an archaeological dig often opens the eyes and minds of the researchers to new possibilities about the past and their implications on the present, so too this process of unearthing the church can open our eyes, forcing us to rethink the narratives we've adopted about how we've gotten to where we are.

In Matt 21:12–14 we read one of the accounts of Jesus clearing out the temple in Jerusalem. There were merchants set up on the temple grounds, selling animals for sacrifice at premium prices, turning sacrifice into commerce, and essentially making the temple grounds into a tourist trap. Jesus had just arrived in Jerusalem with crowds welcoming him and cheering his arrival. They called out to him, "Hosanna to the Son of David! Blessed is he who comes in the name of the Lord!" He was identified by the crowds as a son of King David, as one who came in the name of God, and as a prophet (Matt 21:11).

Immediately after the triumphal entry, Jesus went to the temple. Upon his arrival on the temple grounds, Jesus was moved to anger over what he witnessed. What he saw was people seeking to demonstrate their devotion to God being taken advantage of by merchants and money changers who were motivated more by profit than they were by honoring God. Acting with the authority of God, the power of a king, and the honesty of a prophet, Jesus threw everyone out. This expulsion of the merchants and money changers is accentuated by this phrase from Jesus: "It is written, 'My house shall be called a house of prayer,' but you make it a den of robbers" (Matt 21:13).

If this is how the story ends, it is already astounding. Jesus using his authority as the Son of God to chase the profiteers away is unexpected while at the same time being fully in line with what Jesus' ministry is all about. But what happens after Jesus clears the temple grounds makes clear for us just why Jesus did what he did.

INTRODUCTION

As soon as Jesus ran everyone off, Matt 21:14 says that "the blind and the lame came to him in the Temple, and he healed them."

In order for the temple grounds to be a place where the work of the Lord could be done, Jesus had to get rid of what was getting in the way. The presence of the money changers and merchants and all those who were there to buy and sell—even the presence of the priests and the scribes—served as a deterrent to those who truly wanted to be near God. The religious elites with their ease-of-access to the temple and to the trappings of religious expression had lost sight of why they were there while those who sat on the fringes were acutely aware of their need for God.

This is why we need to unearth the church: when the church makes room for selfishness and human tradition, it does so to the exclusion of both Jesus and those Jesus calls it to serve. When the church rejects self-reflection and Holy Spirit conviction, preferring to point fingers at societal ills as the reason it is struggling, it closes itself off from Jesus and it makes itself unapproachable. When the church refuses to be unearthed, it is refusing to meet the needs of those who are most aware of their needs.

You may have noticed the bulldozer in the cover art for this book. If you have ever watched a skilled operator at work, you'll know both the power and precision they bring to the table with those enormous machines. It can be a brutal and a beautiful thing to watch as they come in and remove everything that needs to be removed and nothing that does not, leaving behind an environment prepared for the next phase.

Brutal and beautiful.

In the work of unearthing the church, both of those descriptors hinge on perspective. Those who are desperate to cling to the selfish, human traditions they have tied to the church will find themselves on their back foot, defensive, and probably angry. The work of unearthing the church is unrelenting. It may seem brutal—savage, cruel, even inhumane—to those experiencing it. That makes sense. To have your preferred image of the church bulldozed and shoved off a cliff hurts. But, on the far side of that which feels brutal—if you hang in there to see what Jesus is doing—your perspective shifts and you are able to observe the beauty of what he's done.

The beauty of freedom from selfishness and human traditions.

The beauty of not relying on yourself.

The beauty of a hope and a life and a church built only on the promises and commands of Jesus.

The beauty of a fresh start.

We are called to pursue just this sort of beauty regardless of the cost; regardless of what needs to be shoved off the cliff in the process.

This idea is implicit in the words of Jesus when he says things like, "You have heard that it was said . . . but I say . . ." (Matt 5:21–22, 27–28, and 31–32) or, "If anyone would come after me, let him deny himself and take up his cross and follow me" (Matt 16:24). Jesus' ministry is pitted against human tradition and selfishness. Jesus' ministry encounters our way of living and forces us to really face what we are doing and why we are doing it. If these aspects of the work of Jesus were applicable to the temple era in which he lived, who do we think we are that they would not be applicable to the church era in which we live?

When I say unearth the church, then, there are two specific things I have in mind; two things that must happen to us. Our foundation must be exposed, and our selfishness must be exorcised.

EXPOSE OUR FOUNDATION

We need to discover what foundation we have built the church on. This requires that we expose our foundation. When we do that we will discover one of two things: one, that Jesus' promises and commands are our foundation or, two, that Jesus' promises and commands are not our foundation. There is no room for pride or defensiveness in this process; those were the reactions that the religious leaders of Jesus' day had to his work and ministry. If pride and defensiveness are our reaction to the unearthing process, that makes the work of exposing our foundation very easy; that

INTRODUCTION

is, if pride and defensiveness are our reactions, Jesus is not our foundation.

EXORCISE OUR SELFISHNESS

With our foundation exposed, we must turn our attention to the stuff we've built on top of the foundation. What ideas, attitudes, and practices have we constructed and are they reflective of the foundation we are supposed to be building on? If we hope to be the church that Jesus founded, we must be built upon Jesus *and* we cannot be built with materials that Scripture does not endorse. When we identify a thought, word, or action that is not in keeping with Jesus as our foundation and Scripture as our guide, we have to drive it out.

Jesus is coming to take us home; however, if we do not want these two things—that our foundation would be exposed and that our selfishness would be exorcised—we should not expect that Jesus is going to want us when he returns. Said differently, if we are not people who desire ongoing reformation, then we are not the people—we are not the church—Jesus is looking for. These two things are an expression of the church's present and future hope—that we would always be in the hands of our Savior, being molded into his likeness, put into action for the advancement of his kingdom, and finally retired into his eternal presence.

As the church undertakes the process of unearthing, there may be a temptation to look at it like a church-growth plan. If that is how you look at it, you are only doubling down on the error that has led the church to its need to be unearthed. Growth is a desirable outcome, but it cannot be the purpose or the focus of the church. If we place our focus on growth, we will miss the same thing the merchants and money changers missed: the people we are called to love and serve and lead to Jesus.

Focusing on growth turns the church into a storefront, Jesus into a packaged good, people into customers, and their presence into profit. This book, then, is not about church growth, it is about reformation. We unearth the church so that we become the church that Jesus calls us to be and so that we serve the people Jesus calls us to serve.

WHO IS THIS BOOK FOR?

This book is for you. I know that sounds a little flippant but stick with me. Whoever you are—whether you are a member of a local church or you are someone who has walked away from the church for various reasons—this book is for you. With that said, whoever you are, this book is intended to accomplish different things in the hands of different people. Let me explain.

First, to the person who has walked away from the church, I am writing to you. Before I say anything else directly to you, I want you to hear this: you have been blamed and bad-mouthed and berated by the church for far too long. Your concerns haven't been considered and your feelings haven't been acknowledged let alone empathized with. I acknowledge the truth of these statements, I acknowledge that I have been part of the reason that you have walked away, and I apologize for myself and on behalf of the church as a whole. This book is for you. This book serves as recognition of the fact that you have legitimate complaints against the church and that we have been far too quick to dismiss you as a quitter or as a deconstructor and far too slow to be curious about your reasons for quitting and deconstructing. This book is an attempt to demonstrate that the church is listening to you, admitting our fault in your departure, and seeking to reconstruct the bridge that led you into the church to begin with.

In your hands, it is my hope that this book will accomplish the work of reconciliation.

My desire is that you would read this book and find in its pages evidence that the church knows it has fallen short of its call. My desire is that you would read this book and discover a self-reflective perspective that demonstrates humility and a desire to do better.

What you will not find in this book, however, is sidestepping the truth of Scripture or a departure from Jesus. In fact, I believe

INTRODUCTION

it is exactly these actions—sidestepping the truth and departing from Jesus—that have been instrumental in the church thinking, speaking, and acting in the ways that have driven you away. As such, this book will identify those departures and invite the church to move back toward Jesus. In that vein, then—as the church is invited to return to Jesus—my hope is that this book will lay some of the groundwork necessary for you to be reconciled with Jesus and with his church and serve as an invitation for you to do just that.

No pressure.

Second, to the person who has been in the church all this time, I am writing to you. Before I say anything else directly to you, I want you to hear this: your efforts for the kingdom of God have been valiant and your heart for the gospel of Jesus has been consistent, but you have gotten a little too comfortable. I know that you have given so much of yourself and spent time working on this project and on that event, but I also know that your spirit hasn't really been in it much of the time. You've been striving and straining and working feverishly to make something—anything—work for the church but it seems like no matter how hard you work nothing seems workable anymore. If we're completely honest, you've probably seriously considered just walking away a time or two yourself. This book is for you. This book serves as an acknowledgment of that which you already know: there is so much wrong with how the church operates, what the church has focused on, and what the church has accomplished. This book is an attempt at speaking to you in that awareness, challenging you to consider where the church has lost track, and inviting you back into the Jesus-given ministry of the church.

In your hands, it is my hope that this book will accomplish the work of conviction.

My desire is that you would read this book and find in its pages a call to return to the person of Jesus and to his bride, the church. My desire is that you would rediscover your connection to Jesus, to your salvation, and to the passion you once held for the kingdom and for the lost.

We've got some digging to do.

A QUICK NOTE

Each chapter from chapter 1 through chapter 10 will end with two "postscripts." These postscripts are brief messages, one to each of the groups identified above, and they will serve as guideposts throughout the book. I offer these postscripts as an attempt to keep us all on the same page, so to speak. Perspective varies from person to person, but if we stay together as we journey, we will all arrive the same place. This is my way of ensuring that no one gets lost along the way.

It would be wonderful if I knew you so that I could address you with your real name when we come to the postscripts. But since I don't know if your name is Alexis or Javier or any of the other millions of possibilities, I am in need of another way to identify you.

So, if you are part of the first group—the group that has walked away from the church or, perhaps, has never been part of the church or has no desire to ever be part of the church—I will address your postscripts to "non-church." This seems like a straightforward description, and I hope that it does not come across as dismissive or condescending. If you are part of the second group—the group that remains connected to the church—I will address your postscripts to "church."

1

Mission Is Revealed by Action

IN MY EARLY TWENTIES I was part of a church that was struggling. Our demographics consisted primarily of people in their seventies and eighties. We were losing members faster than we were gaining them. A long-time pastor had left and his replacement, though respected, was not fully accepted. Factions broke out in the church over what should be done. Citing a community that was rapidly shrinking, some thought it was time to uproot and replant ourselves in a new area. Citing financial strains, some thought it was time to dig our heels in, weather the storm, and play the waiting game.

After long hours of discussion, prayer, and numerous meetings, the church voted by a wide margin to sell the property, uproot, and replant.

Decision made.

However, some members were determined to stay put. A realtor, a lawyer, and a city planner were brought in, each professional explaining that it would be unwise for the church to sell and move in that real estate market and, likewise, it would be malpractice for them—as professionals—to be party to any such plan. The members who brought in the realtor, lawyer, and city planner were successful in scaring the church into reconsidering its decision and so the church stayed where it was and continued its precipitous decline.

Fifteen years later the city approved a development project that pushed the church out of that declining neighborhood and toward what the church had intended to do all those years ago. It found itself in a new neighborhood surrounded by new opportunities for ministry which it met with a revived sense of purpose and hope. Now the church is much healthier, meeting the needs of the new community it is in, and experiencing the peace that comes with being in God's will.

Though this story has a happy ending, a lack of unity in mission and how to accomplish it led the church through a season of hardship. It cannot be known what the future would have held for the church had the voted will of its members been acted upon, but what is apparent is this: the lack of a clear, agreed-upon, and binding mission led to the decay of that church and its influence.

This scenario—hardly unique on the Christian landscape—highlights this important principle: mission is revealed by action.

When a well-intentioned church wants to feel good about itself, the simple task of writing a scripturally sound mission statement often allays concerns of stagnation. "We can't be dying. Look at our mission statement." In such a scenario, the mission statement serves as a smokescreen; a rug under which the church can sweep its missional failings.

There is no such thing as a church that wants to be known as a selfish, self-seeking church much less as a failing church. Every church that has ever existed wants to be seen as a force for good in its community and as a place that is a bastion for the hopeless, helpless, and alone. To that end, when it comes time to have the all-important discussion about mission-making, people come to the table with high and lofty ideas.

"We want to be a Great Commission church. We want to be a church that boldly preaches the gospel." Thinking of Jas 1:22–27 they say, "We want to be a church that meets the needs of the orphan, the widow, and the outcast. We want to be a church that transforms our community."

I want to be clear here: high and lofty are exactly the kinds of ideas we should have when mission-making. The desires expressed in that previous paragraph are precisely the desires that each church should have and that each member of each church should have. The problem comes when, after the mission-making sessions are completed, we are left in the aftermath trying to ascertain how much of that high and lofty idealizing has actually taken root.

WHAT IS THE FRUIT OF THE MISSION-MAKING PROCESS?

If you were to ask someone in your community what your church's mission is, would they be able to tell you? If your church were to cease meeting—cease existing—would anyone outside of your congregation even notice?

The reason each church exists can be seen by evaluating the outcome of their work. That isn't my own framework, by the way. If you want to argue with this conclusion, you're going to have to take it up with Jesus. In Matt 7:17–20 Jesus says that "every healthy tree bears good fruit, but the diseased tree bears bad fruit. A healthy tree cannot bear bad fruit, nor can a diseased tree bear good fruit. Every tree that does not bear good fruit is cut down and thrown into the fire. Thus you will recognize them by their fruits."

Jesus' words here are very straightforward. If you want to know whether a Christian is healthy or unhealthy—or, in this case, whether a church is healthy or unhealthy—you can figure it out in part by examining the results of their actions. Fruit follows action and action follows belief.

Has the gospel been shared? Have people been served? Has God been glorified? These are the kinds of questions that need to be asked in this examination. Ask these questions of yourself and of others in the church. Ask these questions of outside observers. Consider the answers prayerfully.

It is not a wholly productive exercise to evaluate our effectiveness by listening only to the voices of those outside the church; however, it is equally unproductive to listen only to the voices inside the church. If our purpose is to meet the high standard of the Great Commission, then it stands to reason that the perspectives of those who are the object of that commissioning—"all the world," as Jesus says—ought to be considered when they share their perspectives either by speaking them or by simply walking away. One way or the other, they are our fruit.

Bearing in mind that there is only so far that this sort of examination can go—either self-examination or examination based upon the reflections of others—we are left to ask what sort of examination can take us to our destination? Though the answer is obvious, its obviousness is a challenge. While we want to be Scripture-molded churches and followers of Jesus, common wisdom tells us that this approach is part of the problem. "If we steep ourselves deeply in the teachings of Scripture with all of its thou-shalts and thou-shalt-nots," the thinking goes, "don't we run the risk of further marginalizing the population we are called to serve?"

This is the beginning of the unearthing process. Though we must be aware of what those who have walked away from the church have to say, this awareness has to be considered in conversation with our calling. The rubble from which the church needs to be unearthed is comprised of things that have become so much a part of the church that sometimes it can be hard to see where the rubble ends and where the foundation begins.

Yes, consider what those who have walked away from the church have to say about why they've walked away.

No, don't allow that perspective to drag the church away from Scripture.

We should be able to agree on those two statements, but what of the conversation between them? In order for us to be able to consider these two perspectives in conversation, we must first seek to understand them.

POST SCRIPTS

PS to the Non-Church

Mission is a super-common idea in organizational lingo from Fortune 500 all the way to rural churches. The church has long latched onto this concept. They use their mission statement as a litmus test of sorts, holding each idea up against the mission to see if it fits. I'm telling you this because churches take mission-*writing* very seriously, and you—the non-church—are most often the object of those mission statements. That may sound a little strange, to think that a local church in your community is thinking about you, but the church sees it as necessary and as a good thing because they really want you to know the love of Jesus and they're trying to figure out the best way to make that happen.

So, as you think about the idea that mission is revealed by action, think about how the explicit goal of the churches around you is to love you even when they don't do it well (or maybe do it badly). Also, think about how your perspective on the mission and the mission-driven-actions of the church are important to the church, whether the church realizes it or not.

PS to the Church

I know you've been in those meetings, writing up a mission statement, and hoping that this will be the fuel your church needs to really get the rocket of evangelism flying. I also know that you've likely ended up disappointed with the results of these meetings, going from excitement about a mission to disappointment with your church's failure to put the mission into action. Maybe you've been angry with yourself as you come to the realization that once again, just like last time and the time before, even though you said this time would be different, it ended up being the same as always—failure to launch.

This is not an attempt to rub your nose in failures, dragging you back across the landscape of shattered hopes. Instead, this is a challenge to reconsider these failings in light of your scriptural calling. This is not to beat you down for falling short of your mission, but to encourage you to reconnect—or connect for the first time—with Jesus, his mission for you, and the people he's sent you on mission to love and serve.

2

Scriptural Mission

SPECIALIZED TERMINOLOGY CAN BE helpful, but it can also be confusing. This happens because terms used in two different places by two different groups of people often are understood to mean two different things. An extreme example of this in modern American culture is the word "truth." In one place, truth is the expression of an individual's subjective experience. In this case, the word is commonly linked with the word "my" and we get the phrase "my truth." In another place, truth is the expression of an objective fact. In this case, the word is commonly linked with the word "the" and we get the phrase "the truth."

Similarly, the word "mission" as it relates to the church often has different meanings or understandings in different places or at different times. In one place, mission is understood as something the church can do as an extension of itself into the world. In another place, mission is understood as the entire purpose of the church or the reason it exists. The distinction between these two understandings boils down to this: some think of mission as something the church does while others think of mission as why the church exists. This may seem like a small distinction—too small, perhaps, to spend much time on—but this distinction weighs heavily on the work of each individual church.

In your experience with churches over time, you may have noticed this distinction playing out right in front of your eyes, maybe never having given it a second thought.

You walk into a church building and plastered all over the entry way are posters or banners or flyers that invite you to support this mission work or that mission trip. The youth are preparing for a trip to Guatemala. The congregation has been raising funds for wells in the Democratic Republic of the Congo.

Then, you walk into the sanctuary and you hear the worship leader reinforce all of these things that were advertised in the entryway, leading the congregation in prayer for all who are participating in the mission work and for those who will be impacted by the work.

It's all so sincere and lovely and you resonate with the idea of doing as much as you can to support these projects. It is clear that this church has a heart for missionary work and for reaching out to the world for the purpose of meeting needs and showing the love of Jesus.

You walk into another church building and plastered all of the entry way are posters or banners or flyers that invite you to participate in the upcoming church picnic or the seasonally appropriate community festival. The men's group is working on this and the women's group is working on that and the children programs and youth programs are being co-opted to help build and prepare and clean.

Then, you walk into the sanctuary and you hear the worship leader reinforce all of the things that were advertised in the entryway, leading the congregation in prayer for all who are participating in the fellowship activities and for those who will be impacted by the work.

Here too, it is all so sincere and lovely and you resonate with the idea of doing as much as you can to support these projects. It is clear that this church has a heart for fellowship and for the purpose of loving one another and building up the community of Christ.

When considering these two examples side by side, we tend to make a value judgment based upon our understanding of

SCRIPTURAL MISSION

mission—what it is and how it is applied. It is likely, based upon this value judgement, that you would decide the first church is more in line with what the mission of the church is, thus agreeing that mission should be understood as an extension of the church into the world. Its not that you would say that the second church is somehow being sinful or acting inappropriately, but that it may have its priorities mixed up.

This is where the distinction in our understanding of mission becomes volatile. Which church gets it? Which church is doing it right?

Certainly this is an oversimplified example, but the truth of the matter is that this is how churches generally work: one church is focused on the world while the other is focused on itself. I know that sounds a bit abrasive, but lets call it like it is. Churches, like people, are likely to lean into their strengths and they are likely to lean away from the things that make them notice their weaknesses.

The flip side of this oversimplified understanding of churches is this: the first church focuses on missionary efforts—directing its attention outward—because they don't know how to do anything else while the second church focuses on fellowship—directing its attention inward—because they don't know how to do anything else.

As you have likely already determined, the answer to the question about which church is doing it right is that neither of them are doing it right.

There are plenty of places in Scripture that we can turn to in order to get a sense of what the mission of the church is intended to be. I use the word "intended" because the original intention behind the work of the church is critical to understanding what the mission of the church should be. Anything that is created is created with a purpose or an end in mind. If the church was created by Jesus, then it was created for a purpose and if that is the case, then it stands to reason that we should go back to the creation and Creator of the church in order to understand what he intended.

So, of the multiple places in Scripture we can turn, we will start with the words of Jesus in Matt 28:18–20.

"All authority in heaven and on earth has been given to me. Go therefore and make disciples of all nations, baptizing them in the name of the Father and of the Son and of the Holy Spirit, teaching them to observe all that I have commanded you. And behold, I am with you always, to the end of the age."

These are the words Jesus gave to his disciples just before he ascended into heaven following his resurrection. The timing of the instruction elevates its importance to his followers—including his modern followers. These are among the last words his disciples would hear from him in his time on earth—this was his parting shot. With that importance, he talks to his disciples about going, being teachers and baptizers and disciple-makers, being empowered by the Holy Spirit, and being witnesses.

Taken together, these verses paint a clear picture of what Jesus intended for his followers to do. He wanted them to go on the mission of spreading the gospel to the ends of the known world and beyond. He wanted them to take seriously everything that he taught them and to share those things with everyone they encountered.

This sounds very missionary-like. It sounds like we've answered the question about which of the two hypothetical churches got it right. It must be the first one. Jesus sent his disciples—and, by extension, all followers—into the whole world to be witnesses for him and his kingdom. Great! We've got that sorted, so now we can move on to what's next.

Except that it's not quite that simple.

We can't allow the missionary nature of the Great Commission to undermine the content of the Great Commission. Neither can we allow the missionary nature of the Great Commission to undermine the fruit of the Great Commission as it played out in the early church.

Going back, just a moment, to the fact that these are the last words Jesus gave to his disciples, consider this: we must understand the centrality of the Great Commission to the life and work of every Christian, but we must also understand that this missionary instruction was given to the disciples after Jesus had concluded his disciple-making process with them. That is to say, it was not until this point that Jesus determined his disciples to be ready to go and do what this command entails. As such, the Great Commission points backward as much as it points forward; that is, the Great Commission is a culminating point, as much as it is a starting point.

Okay, so now we've got the answer to our question. It is the second of the hypothetical churches that got it right. We need to be focused on teaching and building each other up in the fellowship of the church and the instruction of Jesus. Great! We've got that sorted so, now we can move on to what's next.

You see, it's not so straightforward as to which church is doing it right.

If the final instruction from Jesus points his followers both backward to what he's taught and forward to what they're now supposed to do with what he's taught, then it becomes clear that neither church 1 nor church 2 are doing something wrong, but also that both church 1 and church 2 are under-performing. They're both missing something critical to what the Scripture-prescribed mission of the church is.

Rooting this discussion in Scripture allows us to see how the early church was instructed in their mission as followers of Jesus. Rooting this discussion only in Scripture allows us to avoid—for now—the post-New Testament trappings of church practice. We do not do this at this point to make value judgments about the modern church; rather, we do this to help in unearthing the original image of the church. Since the church is the earthly extension and continuation of the work of Jesus, examining the ministry of Jesus is the logical place to start.

Why did Jesus come? What did Jesus do? What did Jesus accomplish? In order to get at the answers to these questions we will start with John 3:16–17 and Luke 19:10.

"For God so loved the world, that he gave his only Son, that whoever believes in him should not perish but have eternal life. For God did not send his Son into the world to condemn the world, but in order that the world might be saved through him" (John 3:16–17).

"The Son of Man came to seek and to save the lost" (Luke 19:10).

Why did Jesus come? He came to accomplish the work of salvation for those who believe in him. He came in order to provide the way out of eternal death and into eternal life. The primary word of Jesus' ministry, according to John 3:16–17 is salvation, not condemnation and, to that end, Luke 19:10 makes it clear that Jesus came not just to save, but to actively search out those he would save.

What did Jesus do? Boiling this down to just a few things is difficult and, in some ways, a disservice to the work of Jesus. His work and ministry was expansive and multifaceted and likely far more dynamic and charismatic and impactful than a modern Christian might ever think possible. Ephesians 3:20 refers to Jesus as "him who is able to do far more abundantly than all that we ask or think." At the conclusion of the Gospel of John the apostle John declares that "there are also many other things that Jesus did. Were every one of them to be written, I suppose that the world itself could not contain the books that would be written" (John 21:25). In that you begin to see how hard it is to boil it down.

A better question is this: what are the hallmarks of Jesus' ministry? He preached good news, he called people into faith and repentance, and he died on the cross, taking the punishment for the sins of the people he called into faith and repentance. That's certainly not exhaustive, but it is a fair snapshot.

There is a long history of prophetic work in the Old Testament; prophets called by God and sent to the Hebrew people (and, at times, to others—I'm looking at you Jonah) to proclaim God's call to repentance or God's plan for judgment. What makes Jesus' ministry unique, then, is not his call to repentance; rather it is what this call to repentance is paired with.

The good news of the gospel of Jesus is that "if you confess with your mouth that Jesus is Lord and believe in your heart that God raised him from the dead, you will be saved" (Rom 10:9).

SCRIPTURAL MISSION

Earlier in the book of Romans, the apostle Paul describes the gospel itself as "the power of God for salvation to everyone who believes" (Rom 1:16). Jesus called people to a salvation that was marked by faith and repentance and secured by his own death on the cross and resurrection from the dead. This is absolutely unique to the ministry of Jesus.

What Jesus accomplished, then, is the creation and illumination of a path out of sin, death, and hell and into righteousness, life, and heaven. But how does that translate to Christians? What did Jesus expect of his followers? What did he tell them to do? How do we arrive at the claim that the church is the earthly extension and continuation of the work of Jesus?

Jesus told his followers that "whoever believes in me will also do the works that I do; and greater works than these will he do, because I am going to the Father" (John 14:12). Jesus said this to the apostle Philip as part of his response to Philip's request that Jesus show the disciples the Father. Jesus starts off by saying, "Whoever has seen me has seen the Father" (John 14:9) and then in verses 10 and 11 he says, "The words that I say to you I do not speak on my own authority, but the Father who dwells in me does his works. Believe me that I am in the Father and the Father is in me, or else believe on account of the works themselves."

What Jesus is doing is he's making it clear to his disciples that the words he speaks and the works he does are audible and visual manifestations of the invisible God and Father of all mankind. Jesus wants his disciples to be clear on this: he and the Father are one. With that information fresh in their minds, Jesus then tells them that they, too, will do the same kinds of work he has done. The implications of this are super-important: there is work for them to do and they will be empowered to do it. But how?

Using words reminiscent of the Great Commission in Matthew, Jesus told his followers they would receive power when the Holy Spirit comes upon them and they will be his witnesses in all Judea and Samaria and to the end of the earth (Acts 1:8). And this is the "how." Just as Jesus, in unity with the Father, had been sent into the world to preach good news and call people to faith and repentance, so too Jesus' followers, in unity with God the Spirit, have been sent into the world to preach good news and call people to faith. Jesus' vision, expectation, and command to his followers is that they would minister in a way that is consistent with his ministry and they would do this all over the world by the power of the Holy Spirit.

As these statements from Jesus and his words in the Great Commission and the above snapshot of his ministry come together, a fuller picture of Jesus' expectations for his followers and for his church emerges. The question that looms is this: how did the apostles, the early Christians, and the early church put the vision, expectations, and commands of Jesus into practice?

We established earlier that the Great Commission points backward as much as it points forward. The thrust of that statement is that the Great Commission is as much about formation as it is about mission. Said a little differently, Jesus has an interest in both how people become followers as well as in the way people follow.

What evidence is there that the early church took this commissioning seriously? The evidence for this can be broken down into three broad categories: the work of the apostles, the work of the believers, and the results of that work. What follows will be nothing close to an exhaustive exploration of these three branches of evidence, but it will give a sense of the depth of evidence available.

The work of the apostles: On the day of Pentecost—the day that Jesus' promise that the Holy Spirit would come was fulfilled—the apostles were inspired to preach. The Scriptures describes this scene as follows:

> And [the disciples] were all filled with the Holy Spirit and began to speak in other tongues as the Spirit gave them utterance.
>
> Now there were dwelling in Jerusalem Jews, devout men from every nation under heaven. And at this sound the multitude came together, and they were bewildered, because each one was hearing them speak in his own

language. And they were amazed and astonished. (Acts 2:4-7a).

Though the scene confused many of the onlookers, the apostle Peter took center stage and preached a sermon that explained what they were witnessing, declared that Jesus Christ is Lord, convicted the onlookers of sin, and called them to repentance and baptism. He explained that what they saw happening that day was a fulfillment of prophecy (Joel 2:28-32). He noted that in the last days—that is, the days following the coming of the Messiah—God would pour out his Spirit on all people, calling them to conviction, repentance, and salvation.

This bold sermon—seemingly out of character for the man who had denied knowing Jesus at the time of his crucifixion—was incredibly effective. The miraculous works brought on by the moving of the Holy Spirit would continue from this day on throughout the New Testament, but this initial burst—and, notably, this sermon by Peter—yielded about three thousand converts to Christianity.

Much of Acts 13-28 recount the multiple missionary journeys of Paul during which he preached the gospel, established churches, and discipled new believers. Though there was nothing routine about this work, Acts 14:21-23 gives a basic outline of the process the apostles undertook in adhering to the Great Commission.

> When [Paul and Barnabas] had preached the gospel to [the city of Derbe] and had made many disciples, they returned to Lystra and to Iconium and to Antioch, strengthening the souls of the disciples, encouraging them to continue in the faith, and saying that through many tribulations we must enter the kingdom of God. And when they had appointed elders for them in every church, with prayer and fasting they committed them to the Lord in whom they had believed.

Why did Paul and Barnabas go to the city of Derbe? They went in order to participate in the Great Commission of Jesus. They went to make disciples. Why did Paul and Barnabas go back to Lystra, Iconium, and Antioch? They went to encourage and to strengthen the faith of the disciples they had already made in those locations. What did Paul and Barnabas prepare these disciples to do? Paul and Barnabas prepared them for the work of the church by appointing elders to oversee their work and by commissioning them ("they committed them") to the Lord.

What we see through this brief discussion of the work of the apostles is that it was motivated by the Great Commission of Jesus and that it was committed to the development of believers to further the reach of the Great Commission. Paul and Barnabas and Peter and all the others worked to glorify Jesus by being obedient to his commands and by enlisting others to share in the work with them.

The work of the believers: The early Christian community was characterized by commitment. They were committed to prayer, they were committed to study, they were committed to each other, and they were committed to their faith in Jesus. Acts 2:42–47 illuminates this image—one that is both beautiful and hard to imagine in a modern setting—by laying out some of the peculiarities of this community of believers. "Day by day," the Scripture says, they were gathered together, attending the temple together, sharing with each other to the point that no one lacked anything they needed, eating together in each other's homes, and adding more people to the number of converts.

Day by day.

When persecution rose up against Christians, many of these believers were scattered throughout the region. The intended outcome of this persecution and dispersion was that the Christian movement would come to an end. That was not the outcome that occurred. Acts 8:4 puts it succinctly: "Now those who were scattered went about preaching the word." Though they were persecuted and scattered, they—the ordinary, everyday believers—continued to proclaim the gospel of Jesus Christ wherever they went.

The results: There was an explosion of belief in the gospel.

The apostles and all who came to believe in Jesus were faithful in their adherence to the Great Commission and their numbers grew exponentially. When the church of Jerusalem was first starting out, facing little in the way of cultural pushback, they grew in numbers because they were committed to Jesus and his commands. When persecution came upon them, disrupting their lives—and in many cases ending their lives—they grew in numbers because they were committed to Jesus and his commands. Again, Acts puts it succinctly: "So the word of the Lord continued to increase and prevail mightily" (Acts 19:20).

Echoing the highlights of Peter's Pentecost sermon, the teaching that rang out in the early church focused on bearing witness to the work of God, declaring that Jesus Christ is Lord, convicting people of sin, and calling them to repentance and baptism. People's lives were transformed by the gospel and the work of the Spirit. There are many places in the letters of Paul that highlight the result of the work of the apostles and early believers, but 1 Cor 6:11 is particularly poignant as it addresses the believers in Corinth: "But you were washed, you were sanctified, you were justified in the name of the Lord Jesus Christ and by the Spirit of our God."

People were changed.

The early history of the church is marked by the apostles going all over "Judea and Samaria and the end of the earth," but we cannot lose sight of the fact that there are people in each of the locations the apostles traveled who never went anywhere; they stayed in their own towns after receiving instruction from the apostles and they faithfully followed Jesus' instructions by making disciples, baptizing them, and teaching them to observe his commands right where they were. These people were just as obedient to Jesus in their staying as the apostles were in their going. Remember, then, in the early church that both the apostles and those who came to believe in Jesus through their work were all participants in the Great Commission.

This is the first big step in unearthing the church: coming to a clear understanding that the early church understood itself as the continuation and extension of the ministry of Jesus. This can be held up as the standard against which the church measures itself. It is important to note, however, that this is not a declaration that the early church did everything right. There were things that the early church believed, thought, and did that were not in line with the ministry of Jesus and the commissioning of his followers. To be able to believe otherwise, you would need to remove nearly everything in the New Testament from the book of Acts through Revelation.

Even as the church first got off the ground, brokenness started to creep in and the apostles had to teach and encourage and correct again and again. All of Paul's letters were written to churches or individuals that were in need of continued teaching and encouraging and correction. So, we look to the early, formational stage of the church to connect us with what the church of Jesus looked like before centuries of human tradition were overlaid on it, but we do not look to it with a lens that filters out the faults. No, the church is not now and has never been perfect, but it is now and has always been in service of a perfect Savior.

POST SCRIPTS

PS to the Non-Church

There is a heavy dose of the gospel in this chapter. This is intentional for all of the reasons you may be thinking and, hopefully, a couple more reasons as well. It is intentional because I want you to have a chance to hear it clearly without the usual distractions. It is intentional because, ultimately, it is the gospel that is supposed to shape the church's interactions with you and, if that's the case, it only seems fair for you to know what the gospel is supposed to sound and look like. It is intentional because—and this is the hardest bit to admit here—because I know that both the motivations and the actions of the church that you've encountered in your experience may have not made the real gospel of Jesus look too good.

When I outline the fact that the scriptural mission of the church—as summarized in the Great Commission—is both backward focused and future focused, I hope that you hear this: it is focused backward so that those of us who have believed the gospel rely on Jesus for our understanding, motivation, and love, and it is focused forward so that those of us who have believed the gospel will rely on all those same things when we approach you.

PS to the Church

Being able to articulate the gospel is critical. Being able to understand how the gospel impacts you in your formation and in your mission is critical. Being able to see how those two pieces—formation and mission—connect is most critical. These two pieces are a continuation of the themes of the "two churches" from chapter 1; the first church that was mission-minded and the second church that was fellowship-minded. Both mindsets are mission-critical and must be set within a greater mindset that is framed by the overall scriptural mission of the church.

When you think about the scriptural descriptions of the work of the apostles, the work of the early church, and the results of those efforts, do you find yourself inspired, challenged, a little embarrassed, or maybe a little bit of each? If your answer to that series of possible responses is "none of the above," hold that thought for now. We have quite a bit more digging to do.

3

Modern Mission

IN THE BOOK OF Jonah, God tells the prophet Jonah to go to the city of Nineveh and to tell the people of the city that God has seen their wickedness and has decided to destroy them. Fast-forward past Jonah running in the opposite direction that God tells him to go, past Jonah nearly drowning in the sea only to be swallowed by a big fish, and past Jonah's repentance. After Jonah delivers the message that God told him to give, Jonah sets up camp on a hillside outside the city, excited to witness the destructive work of a righteous God.

It is tempting—easy even—to stand on a hillside outside the city, examining and judging the modern church for all of its shortcomings. That judgmentalism is a place in which many hearts have been hardened and from which many attacks have been launched. The heart behind that stance had been a constant companion of mine for a number of years as I lamented a lack of vision, a lack of commitment, a lack of faith, and a lack of growth in the church. These observations culminated in this judgment that I shared on Facebook in 2016:

"Perhaps the best thing that could happen to the church in America is that all our buildings be demolished."

I'm not ashamed to have made that post: it was an honest reflection at a moment in my life when I was feeling frustrated and powerless in the face of what seemed like quickly shifting attitudes about the church and participation in the church. So, I am not ashamed to have shared an honest reflection; I am, however, ashamed that *that* was my honest reflection. I am ashamed that my concerns and fears for the church led me to postulate that it would be a good thing for nearly four hundred thousand buildings to be destroyed.

Going back to Jonah's story for a moment, as it turned out, the people of the city of Nineveh were so convicted by the message Jonah delivered that the entire population of the city, all the way up to the king himself, repented and turned their lives around. They began to worship God. God relented on his judgment and he spared the city. The people of Nineveh praised God for his mercy.

In the face of such a miraculous turn of events, it is reasonable to expect that Jonah would have joined the people of Nineveh in praising God for his mercy, grateful that God had used him to bring a message to the people that led to their repentance and forgiveness. This is the goal of any prophet and, you could imagine, any prophet would be overjoyed to have his message received and heeded. But this is not what Jonah did.

Jonah's words in Jon 4:3 make it clear that he was so displeased with God's mercy—that he was so desirous of Nineveh's destruction—that he would rather die than live. In his own words, "now, O Lord, please take my life from me, for it is better for me to die than to live." Jonah stood on the mountain, his heart full of judgment for the people God had just spared, and he seethed in anger and self-pity. Why? Because he didn't get his way.

As I said, it is tempting—even easy—to stand on a hillside outside the city, examining and judging. Sometimes we can get so wrapped up in correction and in justice that all we can see is the burning, white-hot judgment that unrighteous, unwashed, and unrepentant people need. We may even "say our piece" in anger as we walk out the door, convinced that those people deserve what's coming to them. Then we sit back, watch, and wait for the implosion. So tempting and so easy. But not helpful or holy, especially not in light of the fact that God's trademarks are redemption and restoration.

As we examine the modern church, then, it is not the goal of this chapter to take cheap shots or point fingers or even to bring a word of condemnation. We should not imitate the errors of Jonah. We should not go down the easy, self-satisfying path of social media obliteration. Instead, we should make sober observations about modern church culture and we should receive this as an invitation into self-reflection and, as necessary, into repentance so that we can be redeemed and restored.

WHAT DOES IT LOOK LIKE THE MISSION OF YOUR CHURCH IS?

We will go more in depth on this question when we come to the chapters on the outside-in and inside-out evaluation phases, but for now let's consider what is necessary in order to answer this question. Though Jonah's attitude was inappropriate and unhelpful, Jonah's progression through his interactions with Nineveh gives us a model to consider. We start with a perspective about the church, we get up close and personal with the church, then we step back again and consider what we had right, what we had wrong, and what about our attitude and approach needs to change. Jonah did not come out of this exercise changed because he concentrated on his own perspective. If we hope to do better than Jonah, we have to set our perspective aside—as much as possible—and lean on God's perspective as outlined in Scripture.

So, what do you see when you take a look at the church? Whether you are coming from an insider's perspective or an outsider's perspective, what do you see? Some of these observations are superficial, such as what you actually observe with your eyes. Some of these observations are more substantive, such as what is revealed by polls, surveys, or studies. None of these observations paints a complete picture, but all of them—both independently and as a whole—help in focusing in on the complete picture.

1. Both the parking lots and the pews are much emptier than they used to be
2. There aren't very many eighteen- to thirty-four-year-olds in the church (only about 14 percent)
3. There are lots of folks in the sixty-five-plus range in the church (at least 42 percent)
4. The pastors are getting older (average age of 57)
5. Pastors aren't trustworthy (52 percent of the non-church believe this)
6. The church is judgmental (44 percent of millennials believe this)
7. The church is detached (52 percent of millennials believe this)

The first of these observations (1) is strictly anecdotal based upon my observations and the observations others have shared with me over the last few years. It is important to note that this observation comes in the aftermath of the COVID-19 pandemic and that there are many aspects of pre-pandemic life that have not yet rebounded. With that said, anyone who has spent significant time in church both pre and post COVID-19 will have noticed this marked shift. There are fewer cars and fewer people in the pews and the initial burst of returns following the pandemic has slowed to a stand-still. As of now, it doesn't seem that anyone else is itching to come back.

The next three of these observations (2, 3, and 4) come from a 2020 survey of churches.[1] The population of local congregations—and the leadership thereof—is aging rapidly. Comparing these numbers to where they were just a quarter of a century ago makes the reality of aging even more stark. It has always been the case that those in the sixty-five-plus set were the backbone of local congregations in terms of wisdom and experience and encouragement, but their role as the primary demographic to such an extent is new and expanding.

---

1. Thumma, *Twenty Years of Congregational Change.*

The final two of these observations (5 and 6) are from opinion polling that provide a snapshot, in part, of the reasons why a shrinking number of adults (especially those in the twenty-two to thirty-six millennial age range) participate in the church.[2] A large percentage are convinced that the church doesn't care about what's most important to them (detached) and that the church is far more concerned with being right than with being loving (judgmental).

Church, you can have your opinions about these perspectives, but until you are willing to face these perspectives, understanding that your job isn't first to correct but to hear, then you will make no headway in changing their perspective on the church or on the gospel. You will not "fix" someone's perspective by telling them how wrong you think they are. This is something that can only be addressed by giving them a new experience that challenges their previous experience.

In chapter 1, looking at the importance of the terminology that we use and coming to agreed upon definitions, I referenced the terms "*my* truth" and "*the* truth." Here is where those terms meet us in this discussion. No matter what "the truth" of the gospel and the work of the church is intended by God to be, the only truth that most folks will ever believe is the truth that is presented to them in their own experiences. The truth of the gospel is that it is good news, that it is the only means of forgiveness for the sins that we've committed, and that it is the perfect demonstration of the grace of God through the work of Jesus Christ. All of that is true *and* it is true that if someone's experiences with the church and with Christians have shown them that both the church and Christians are mean-spirited, only interested in being right, and not willing to listen, then the truth of *that* experience will trump the truth of God's intention.

It is important to note that this is simply how perceptions work. No matter what is true, if the truth is not communicated clearly, what becomes true in the mind of the observer is what they have observed. And, can you blame them? Does it make sense to

---

2. Nieuwhof, "What Non-Christian People Really Think."

expect someone to come to believe something that is contrary to what their experiences have shown them? No, of course not.

What Christians demonstrate as members of the church and representatives of the gospel becomes the truth for those who experience the church and the gospel through them. The responsibility, then, falls on the members and representatives and not on those who observe.

What does the mission of your church appear to be to outside observers? As you consider your perspective on your church—both when you're in a good mood and when you're in a bad mood—what do you think your church is communicating to your community? Are you willing to consider the perspectives of those outside of your church as potential sources of truth *about* your church's witness, ministry, and reputation?

This is not an invitation to approach the church like Jonah approached Nineveh—hoping for wholesale destruction—but an invitation to see the church for how it is perceived, see it for what it actually is, and then to participate in God's work of restoration

POST SCRIPTS

PS to the Non-Church

This will be a recurring theme throughout the book: what you think and how you see things matters to the church. I know that there is a danger here at coming across as patronizing or mechanical, but that is just the nature of empathy and reflective listening (especially in written form). The citations of polls and surveys are an attempt to actually listen to your perspectives and to hold them up against the church's self-perceptions. This is also a challenge to the church to acknowledge the reality of different perspectives.

There is no way of knowing if you personally resonate with the six "surface-deep" observations about the church from this chapter, but they are offered here as an open hand; as a way of saying that these are things the church must recognize about how it is and/or how it is perceived *and* that the church is ready to hear what you might offer in addition.

PS to the Church

How you see yourself, how you are seen, and how you actually are—these are often three distinct things. We always hope that there is little to no distinction, but it only takes a little conversation and a little prayer for us to realize just how distinct they are. If our desire is to have integrity—that is, for who we are and both how we see ourselves and how others see us to be integrated—then we need to start by being willing to listen.

As Jesus is speaking to the church in Laodicea, he offers them this perspective: "For you say, I am rich, I have prospered, and I need nothing, not realizing that you are wretched, pitiable, poor, blind, and naked" (Rev 3:17). What they saw in themselves was very different than what the reality was. But, Jesus did not make this assessment as a final judgment; it was a call out of their lack of integrity. "Those whom I love, I reprove and discipline, so be zealous and repent" (Rev 3:19).

So church, be zealous and repent.

4

Outside-In

TOWARD THE END OF the previous chapter I offered a series of questions for you to wrestle with:

1. What does the mission of your church appear to be to outside observers?

2. As you consider your perspective on your church—both when you're in a good mood and when you're in a bad mood—what do you think your church is communicating to your community?

3. Are you willing to consider the perspectives of those outside of your church as potential sources of truth *about* your church's witness, ministry, and reputation?

In engaging with these questions it is important to consider them deeply and prayerfully in light of two particular things: first, in light of the perspective of those to whom the church is sent and, second, in light of how scriptural-reflection and self-reflection address that perspective.

So, before we can move to scriptural-reflection and self-reflection, we need to spend some time engaging in the perspective of those to whom the church has been sent. We will get at that perspective, first, by identifying the who—who Jesus has sent the church to encounter—second, by asking questions of them, and third, by listening to understand their answers.

It may occur to some in the church that we ought to start from the other perspective, thinking first about what Scripture has to say and going on to engage with our communities and their perspectives from there. "Aren't we supposed to bring the scriptural perspective to our communities, not their perspective to the church?"

A couple of things to note here about that question:

First, those of us who are in the church know that if we are formed by the power of the Holy Spirit and are becoming more and more Christlike in the way that we think, speak, and act, it is impossible for us to leave the scriptural perspective behind. So, even as we solicit the perspective of our community for consideration, we do so from a place of already being formed by the Spirit.

Second, one of the greatest errors of the modern church—the church in America in particular—is the expectation of Christlike behaviors and lifestyles from people who have no relationship with Jesus. That is to say that the church often starts from a position of judgmentalism toward people who haven't yet submitted to Jesus as Lord.

I took four years of Spanish in my middle and high school years. Now, some decades later, I retain bits and pieces of what I learned, but it is mostly gone. Yet as I was learning, my teachers were kind and encouraging with an eye toward growth in my comprehension and speaking of Spanish. They knew that I was starting from a place of zero understanding, and so, they were gracious with me, not expecting me to know things that I hadn't been taught and giving me room to try, make mistakes, and then try again.

It would have been unkind and utterly discouraging if, as I was in the infancy of my learning, my teachers had berated me for my lack of knowledge, asking me, "Why don't you understand this already? This is elementary stuff." It would have been worse had those teachers berated me for my lack of knowledge if I wasn't even taking the class, showed no interest in learning, and had no foundational understanding of the language. In that circumstance, who among us would approve of the behavior of those teachers?

Or, consider a baby, eight to ten months old, taking her first crack at walking. She crawls to a chair and, using all her might, slowly and methodically inches her way upward, pulling with her arms and pushing with her legs. After several moments of extreme exertion, she finds herself fully upright, her little legs quivering under the weight of this new posture. A second or two passes and her legs give way, she tumbles to the floor, and she turns her head to you for a sign as to how she should react to this fall.

What do you do? Do you yell at the baby, chastising her for being weak and incapable of walking, making her feel half-an-inch tall for failing so miserably at walking? Or, do you stoop down at her side with a smile, telling her that she's done a good job—made a wonderful attempt at walking—and offer her a hand to help lift her back off the floor for another attempt, this time with a little assistance?

A teacher who berates a pupil for not knowing what he hasn't learned and a person who yells at a baby for her inability to walk; these are unflattering characteristics to which none of us would aspire. And yet, it is this attitude that we Christians are often guilty of in our interactions with folks outside of the church, treating people as though they should be fluent in the ways of Christianity and the church even before they've been introduced to what Christianity and the church actually is. Ironically, in treating people this way, we in the church often reveal ourselves to be guilty of the same thing we accuse the unchurched of being—un-Christlike and sinful.

We start, then, from the perspective of the community because what they see, how they experience us, and what they have to say about those things matters. We open up a dialogue so that we can understand the disconnect and, in doing so, give ourselves the best chance of reconnecting. If we don't first listen, what right do we have to expect to ever be listened to ourselves? If we don't first seek to understand, is it reasonable for us to hope to be understood?

Just in case the notions of "first listen" and "first seek to understand" don't resonate, consider God's posture toward us: "We love because God first loved us" (1 John 4:19). God, already fully aware of our thoughts and intentions, loved us and he demonstrated that love for us "in that while we were still sinners Christ died for us" (Rom 5:9). Since that's the case and since the call upon the Christian is to become more Christlike as we grow in faith and grace and understanding, then it makes sense that we should have a posture of love toward those outside of the faith *and* a desire to get to know their thoughts and intentions and that we would *still* love them *after* their thoughts and intentions are known.

WHO DID JESUS SEND THE CHURCH TO ENCOUNTER?

In our discussion of the mission of the church we identified this group broadly as the people in "Jerusalem and in all Judea and Samaria, and to the end of the earth" (Acts 1:8). This description is sufficiently broad so as to encapsulate all the people in all the world who were not yet believers in Jesus.

While this is a fair description—it is, after all, the group that Jesus references in sending believers into the world—it leaves some room for specificity that would be helpful in our context. For our purposes, we can understand the objects of the evangelistic work of the church in three categories: those who have never heard of Jesus, those who have heard of Jesus but rejected him, and those who have come to know Jesus and then walked away from him.

The first group—those who have never heard of Jesus—might be thought of as unreached. This demographic is precious in the eyes of Jesus and the church has been sent to them to love them and to teach them the truth and commands of Jesus. The second group—those who have heard of Jesus but rejected him—might be thought of as unrepentant. This demographic is precious in the eyes of Jesus and the church has been sent to them as well.

The last group—those who have come to know Jesus and/or his church and have walked away—might be thought of as "done." In fact, the term "dones" is how this group is often referred to in research and writings. This demographic is precious in the eyes of Jesus and the church has been sent to them as well. This group will be our primary focus in considering the outside-in perspective, in part because this group somewhat represents all three groups at the same time.

In some instances, the "dones" are people who wish now that they had never heard the name of Jesus; that they had been left unaware of the church and the kingdom of God and permitted to live their lives as though none of that was up for consideration. In other instances, the dones are people who wish now that they had never accepted what it was that the church offered them; that they would have heard and then immediately rejected the church and everything it was offering because the result for them has been pain and heartache.

When I talk about those who are identified as or have identified *themselves* as "dones," I do so with compassion and sorrow in equal measures. Compassion because the pain many of them have experienced at the hands of the church is real, and sorrow because the pain they've experienced is often the result of people representing Jesus badly.

This is a group that has been identified and studied and poked and prodded in books and in articles, in podcasts and on social media. This is a group that is often considered to be the "holy grail" for the church—the group that, if the church can just get the right formula, will lead the American church from its precipitous twenty-first-century decline into a new, twenty-first-century ascension.

Speaking directly to those who may identify with this group in one way or another: even though it is true that I would love to see all of you come back to Jesus (that is, if you walked away from Jesus when you walked away from the church) and return to the church, the goal in this chapter is to understand who you are and to hear what you have to say so that the church has a chance to face the ways in which you feel the church has failed. My prayer is that we would face these failings, repent of any sin, seek forgiveness from God and from you, and perhaps have another opportunity to be the church and to show you the church Jesus calls us to be.

WHO ARE THE DONES?

There is no way to draw a sweeping picture that adequately encompasses all who might be described as or who might self-describe as "done." Dones are women, men, Hispanic, black, white, straight, LGBT, Republican, Democrat, Eagles fan, Cowboys fan, you name it. They are rich and they are poor. They are well-connected and they are cut off. This cultural phenomenon has left no demographic untouched. According to recent statistics, 16 percent of the US population has stopped going to church since the beginning of the COVID-19 pandemic—13 percent of millennials, 15 percent of Gen X, and 22 percent of boomers.[1]

So, perhaps the question of "who?" is less helpful than the question of "why?" Why did they leave? Similar to the question of "who?" there is no way to draw a sweeping picture that adequately encompasses all of the reasons why.

- Many have left because life circumstances changed.
- Many have left because of COVID-19 shutdowns.
- Many have left because their questions or doubts were dismissed.
- Many have left because of trauma or hurt they experienced in the church.

Those first two groups might be described as accidental or incidental departures; that is, they had no expressed intent in leaving, it just sort of happened. Those who are part of the third and fourth category—those who felt dismissed and those who experienced church-caused trauma or hurt—left the church intentionally.

---

1. "New Chapter in Millennial Church."

This group of dones—those who left because of the way churches treated them—have a wide and varied array of experiences in the church. Some had been lifelong church members, born and raised in the church and deeply entrenched in the ways of the church. Some were late to the game, coming to the church after a life crisis or a philosophical awakening.

Their points of connection with the church world are just as varied as their reasons for leaving. Some left because the church seemed intolerant of certain people. Some left because a church member spoke about them behind their back and they found out about it. Some left because a pastor or leader was exposed as an abuser. Some left because they themselves were abused.

Neither of these characterizations—who left and why they left—are exhaustive, but these lists begin to shine a light on the variety of people and experiences within this community. The hurt that was caused—itself often enough to forever sour their appetite on the church—was often doubled-down on by those in the church, as many folks in the church poured insult on top of harm.

I have a friend—we'll call her Angela—who has long since left the church behind her. Angela grew up in a typical Christian home with parents who, themselves, had grown up in Christian homes. As she describes her upbringing, she says that they were more nominal in their faith than committed; that is, they called themselves Christian but didn't attend any church regularly. When Angela reached her teenage years and began to ask questions about the faith she had been raised with, her questions were often dismissed by the adults around her as unimportant or as "matters of faith that you just have to believe," to quote her. As her questions were dismissed, she began to feel dismissed and disconnected.

This feeling of disconnection grew into a chasm between Angela and her parents and ultimately between Angela and her church. Speaking to her pastor one Sunday she recalls saying to him, "I want to believe, I really do. I just don't understand why everyone treats me like I'm sinning by asking questions. It's like you're saying, 'God can't handle it.'"

His response to Angela was straightforward: "Maybe your questions just mean you don't actually have faith."

This, for her, was the last blow to her faith; that she was treated with hostility for exploring the questions she had about the faith that she had inherited from her parents. She left and never looked back.

This is a psychological harm that is often caused by the church.

Imagine for a moment that you have a bank account with a large balance, say $100,000. You've been setting money aside for years for a down payment on a house and you are nearing the end of the savings phase, getting ready for the big purchase. Out of the blue, you get a notification from the bank that this account now has a negative balance of −$118.87. You go to your spouse and ask if they know anything about this. They don't.

You call the bank and speak to customer service, demanding to know what happened to your money. The customer service representative tells you they don't have an answer for you and suggest you go to your local branch. You go to the bank and speak to an account specialist who, without looking at the computer or making any phone calls, looks at you and says, "Why are you asking all these questions? Why can't you just trust us?"

Feeling dismissed and taken advantage of, the likely course of action you would take is that you would remove all of your business from this bank and then pursue legal action for their mishandling of your accounts. You would leave and never look back.

And yet, this is essentially how the church often treats people when it comes to questions about faith. This story that Angela shared is repeated over and over in the lives of people—often in late teens or early adulthood—who, out of a desire to understand more deeply and to learn how to address their questions in a way that is mature and faithful to Scripture, reach out to those who are older and more mature in the faith and ask.

I can hear some people saying in their minds right now—and I know this is the case because I've heard it in conversation—"Why didn't she just go to another church?" Or, maybe you're thinking, "Well, that's not the response she would have gotten from me"?

Let's address these common responses.

"Why didn't she just go to another church?"

Though the basic premise to this question seems reasonable—that she might have found a different sort of response in a different church—the underlying implication places blame on the one who left. By asking that question, what we are really doing is agreeing with the pastor who told her that she didn't actually have faith because, if she *did* have faith, she would have continued to search for the answers.

Why is it the tendency, so often, for us in the church to question the motivations of the ones who ask questions as opposed to questioning our own motivations and actions?

In Rom 10:14 the apostle Paul asks these questions of believers (that is, church members): "How then will they call on him in whom they have not believed? And how are they to believe in him of whom they have never heard? And how are they to hear without someone preaching?"

The burden in these circumstances, according to Scripture, is on those of us in the church. Working backward in that verse, it is up to Christians to preach so people can hear so people can believe so people can then call on the Lord and be saved. Preaching is the proclamation of the truth of God, whether from a pulpit or in a conversation. Preaching, then, is also found in answering the sincere questions of someone struggling to believe.

We should—and I use that word with as much weight as possible—we *should* be patient without end in answering questions about faith. If my friend's pastor all those years ago was tired of the questions or if he had run out of patience for my friend or if he simply didn't have the answers she was looking for, his response to her never should have been what it was; rather, he should have looked at her and said, "I'm not sure I've got the answers you're looking for, but I'd like a chance to find someone who does."

Asking "Why didn't she just go to another church?" blames her, accuses her of the same thing her pastor did, and unhooks the church from any responsibility and accountability.

"Well, that's not the response she would have gotten from me."

I don't know you so I'm not going to assume this is a lie. Instead, I'd just challenge you to consider that this is a defensive and dismissive response. The primary concern in this story is that of the eternal destiny of the person asking the questions. The one who needs to be ministered to and defended is the one who was seeking the truth and was cut off at the pass, not the pastor who failed her or the church he hides in. Further, it is dismissive in that it relegates her experience to the category of anecdote. This allows us to treat her hypothetically rather than as a real person dealing with real spiritual questions.

These two responses are the backbone of the church's defensiveness in the face of many of these stories.

"They could have gone somewhere else."

"That's not how I would have treated them."

These responses further harm the individual struggling in their faith. These responses further harm the person who has been dismissed as faithless. These responses further harm the ones who, their whole lives, were taught that church is a place of love. These responses, carelessly spoken, implicate the entirety of the church—every congregation and every pastor everywhere—in the harm that any congregation or any pastor anywhere has ever caused.

Fair or unfair, this is the implication.

What's more, Angela's story is relatively benign when compared to the horrors many have faced at the hands of the church. There are certain curtains we don't want to look behind, certain closets we do not want to look inside because of what we know is hiding there. You likely know what I am alluding to here. My aim is not to be graphic or sensational, but this is part of the harm that we need to face and contend with.

Sexual misconduct or sexual abuse perpetrated by church members and church leadership has wracked the church and

Outside-In

its influence for decades. A study done in 2019, the year before COVID-19 exploded onto the scene, found that 10 percent of Protestants under the age of thirty-five decided to leave the church because they did not feel that abuse allegations were taken seriously. Additionally, 9 percent of that same group said they left the church because they, themselves, did not feel safe from sexual abuse. Another 14 percent said that they decided to change where they attended church due to unwanted sexual advances, and 23 percent of this same group (those aged eighteen to thirty-four) said they know someone in the church who has been the victim of abuse, sexual or otherwise.[2]

These statistics bring greater clarity to the breadth and depth of the problem the church is facing. These statistics paint a picture of the way the church is viewed by many people who have left. These statistics paint a picture of the way in which the media—social, mainstream, and otherwise—portrays the church. This is the outside-in view of the church that those of us in the church need to see, believe, and seek to understand.

Does any of this mean that the church is utterly corrupt and beyond saving? Certainly not. Jesus himself said that the gates of hell will not prevail against the church (Matt 16:18) and, since that's the case, that would seem to mean that church is also unable prevail against itself. Why? Because the church is founded and upheld by God's mighty right hand.

So, no, the church is not utterly corrupt and the church is not beyond saving; however, we must be willing to acknowledge that there is corruption within the church and that this corruption has caused serious, long-lasting, and—in some cases—irreparable harm to some of the people Jesus calls the church to serve.

When confronted with the task of unearthing the church in the face of this reality, the church must feel the weight of the burden it bears. In order for us to be able to even begin approaching those who are on the outside looking in, we have to first be willing to consider their perspective.

---

2. Earls, "Churchgoers Split on Existence."

When presented with an image of the church that is unflattering, it is a disservice to just dismiss it in favor of a preferred image. Everyone involved would love to simply default to a better, friendlier, rosier image of the church. The problem is that none of that starry-eyed pretending goes any distance to addressing the real image that is laying before all of us.

Regarding these things, the work of unearthing the church looks like this: listen to those who have been harmed, seeking to understand their perspective, considering their stories against the backdrop of the church that Jesus established, and in the instances wherein hurt has been caused because the church has failed to live up to that image, the church must repent and seek to set things right.

POST SCRIPTS

PS to the Non-Church

At the risk of backtracking on one of the primary points from this chapter, even though it is unrealistic and unfair to expect you to abide by the teachings of the church or to have a deep understanding of the teachings of the church, it is neither unrealistic nor unfair to recognize that you likely have a basic understanding of the church's moral expectations and demands. It's fair to say this because American culture and law is still underpinned by many of these basics expectations. What is both unfair and unrealistic on the part of the church is the general expectation that those in the church have that everyone in society should just go along to get along.

More important are the ways in which the church fails its own test, expecting you who do not have a moral commitment to the teachings of Jesus to comply with them even when the church—its membership and its leadership—seem to regularly fail at living up to the same standard. This point is not lost, and the hypocrisy it illuminates is good reason for you to be skeptical of the church in general.

PS to the Church

How many stories like Angela's have you heard? How many of those stories have been from people that you know personally and are still in relationship with? I have heard many such stories, but Angela is one of only a few people I know who have left the church and with whom I am in somewhat regular contact. I share this here as a confession of sorts—I feel I should have many more such relationships—but I also share this here because my guess is that you don't know many if any more "Angelas" than I do.

Why is that the case?

Is it because folks who have left the church aren't often in relationship with people who are still in the church? Doubtful.

Is it because you aren't often in relationship with people who have left the church? This is also doubtful.

The reason this is the case is not because of a lack of relationships, but because of a lack of intimacy in relationships. We need to do a better job of getting to know people by caring about their whole story and listening to both what they are sharing and what they are withholding.

5

Inside-Out

COMING OUT OF THAT last chapter, considering the perspectives of those who have gone out of the church—specifically of those who have been harmed by the church in one way or another—those of us *in* the church are left with many things to consider. If we take the evaluation at face value, believing it to be an honest reflection of the way in which people have been treated and have experienced their treatment, we need to be willing to consider the following questions about ourselves:

1. How do these criticisms hit us?
2. Are these criticisms fair and, perhaps more fundamentally, how can we know if they are fair?
3. What is the fruit of our work as a church?

This is a call to an inside-out evaluation. We started with the outside-in perspective so that we would have something to wrestle with, something to consider alongside what we see in ourselves and what the Scriptures have to say about both of those things (what others see and what we see).

Critical self-evaluation is a difficult task to undertake in many cases because we, as our own subject, tend to be far more gracious and forgiving of ourselves than we would be of others. Admittedly, there is a contingent of people and organizations that are self-flagellating, looking for any excuse to second-guess and berate themselves. The truth of the matter often lies in the middle; the intervening space between what we see in ourselves and what others see in us.

In this chapter, then, we will consider what it is that we see in ourselves in light of the less-than-flattering revelations of the previous chapter.

In Jas 1:22–24 the brother of Jesus shares the following analogy:

> But be doers of the word, and not hearers only, deceiving yourselves. For if anyone is a hearer of the word and not a doer, he is like a man who looks intently at his natural face in the mirror. For he looks at himself and goes away and at once forgets what he was like.

As Christians—and as a church—we find our identity in Christ and in his revealed word, the Bible. That is to say, we are only who we are supposed to be to the degree that we live in accordance with what the Scriptures teach. We can only know who we are supposed to be, who we are, and how we measure up so long as we keep the word of God in our hearts and minds.

Mirrors are not new technology nor is the idea behind them. People have seen themselves in reflections for as long as there has been still water to sit beside. Photography is far newer on the grand timescale, but it is by no means new in the eyes of modern civilization. Put that alongside the selfie culture that we inhabit and we can say with confidence that nearly everyone is familiar with what they, themselves, look like. We all know the basic features of our own faces; the shape of our eyebrows, the spacing between our nose an our lips, the color of our eyes and hair, and so on. No one looks in the mirror at any given moment and is shocked by what they see (disappointed, perhaps, but not shocked).

What would be startling is if, when looking in the mirror, you do not appear the way you thought you would.

What James is saying in these verses is that those of us who hear the word of God but do not do the word of God are like people who are shocked when they look into the mirror and see themselves. Somehow, between glances, they have forgotten entirely what they look like and, thinking they appear other than they do, are startled when faced with reality once again.

James continues in 1:25 saying, "But the one who looks into the perfect law, the law of liberty, and perseveres, being no hearer who forgets but a does who acts, he will be blessed in his doing."

Rather than walking away from the reflection—or the word of God—and forgetting what we've seen, James is saying that the true Christian is the one who remembers and does what the word of God says in between hearings.

When we engage in the process of self-evaluation, then, we do so mostly because we want to see the honesty of reflection. When we peer into the word of God it reflects to us what God desires to see in us, not what we desire to see in ourselves.

This is one of the primary reasons that self-evaluation is so often avoided; it is because we do not want to come face-to-face with the ways in which we are failing or falling short. This is also a primary reason we often recoil at criticism; it is because we'd rather hold onto our own flattering self-perception as opposed to having to deal with the possibility that what others see in us is a more accurate representation of reality.

So, how do the criticisms from the outside-in perspective hit us?

Well, start with what the criticisms are. The church has often been dismissive of questions asked by seekers, questioning their sincerity and their faith. The church has been perpetrators of or apologists for abuse and abusers of various kinds against people who had trusted the church to care for them. The church has caused harm to people in various ways and, instead of seeking ways to create healing, has often doubled-down on dismissiveness, abuse, and harm.

Once we get passed the initial defensiveness that is bound to rise up at hearing these criticisms, how do these criticisms land?

The truth of the criticisms is undeniable. Most, if not all of us within the church can likely identify either a testimony that we've heard or a news story that we've come across that exemplifies these criticisms. Many of us likely have an up close and personal story that we can share that testifies to the truth of these criticisms.

Since this is the case, the way that these criticisms should land in our heart and minds is with sadness—sadness over the hurt the church has caused and sadness over the damage this has inflicted on the preaching of the gospel and the advancement of the kingdom of God. This is a sorrow that should drive us back to the perfect image of the church laid out in the word of God, leading us to wonder about the ways in which our reflection is falling short of that perfect image.

Are these criticisms fair and, perhaps more fundamentally, how can we know if they are fair?

What is the intended outcome of the preaching of the gospel? When members of the church live out the word of God, what is the hoped-for result? What is the result that the Bible outlines?

Jesus, quoting the prophet Isaiah, said the following about himself and his ministry:

> The Spirit of the Lord is upon me, because he has anointed me to proclaim good news to the poor. He has sent me to proclaim liberty to the captive and recovering of sight to the blind, to set at liberty those who are oppressed, to proclaim the year of the Lord's favor. (Luke 4:18-19)

This is the ministry that Jesus came to fulfill and the type of ministry that the church is intended to perpetuate. Jesus' intention for his followers was that we would follow him in obedience, being an authentic reflection of his character into the world.

Are we proclaiming good news?

Are we calling people into the liberty of Christ?

Are we setting oppressed people free?

Are we declaring the fact that there is favor for those who are in Christ?

It is likely that many of us can answer in the affirmative to these questions. Most of us can think of many ways in which we have participated in this type of ministry. And yet, as we noted before, most of us can also think of times when these things haven't happened, when the opposite of these things have happened. We can think of instances when the good news was supplanted by a message of condemnation or when people have been oppressed by guilt for their brokenness rather than forgiveness for their sins or when people have been burdened with the notion of having to earn God's favor through good works and pure lives.

To the degree that these outcomes are not realized—or, worse, to the degree that an inverse outcome results—these criticisms are fair. I can sense the urge within us to continue to say, "But that's not how we act. That's not how we treat people. That's not what our church is like."

When I was thirteen I had to have blood work done. This was my first experience with that process and I was a little scared but very intrigued. I settled into my seat and proceeded to watch as the nurse wrapped the band around my upper arm, wiped the skin above the target vein, and inserted the needle. As I watched this, I felt little beads of sweat bubble up on my forehead, I sensed my heart rate rapidly increasing, I noticed gray and then black creep into my peripheral vision, and then I woke up several minutes later laying down on a bed.

The summer between high school and college I had to get a few vaccinations to meet the requirements for admission. I went to the health department and, after waiting a few minutes, was called back to face the gauntlet. I sat down in the chair and received my three vaccinations. After the third vaccination hit my arm I felt little beads of sweat bubble up on my forehead, I sensed my heart rate rapidly increasing, I noticed gray and then black creep into my peripheral vision, and then I woke up several minutes later laying down on a bed.

To this day, now two or three decades later, every time I have to get blood work done I look the other way, sure that if I watch the process I will pass out. Every time I get a vaccination, I get nervous that I am going to pass out. Even though I have had my blood drawn countless times since I was thirteen and even though

INSIDE-OUT

I have had many vaccinations since I graduated high school, I have never passed out again. And yet, I still get nervous, expecting the experiences of my past to repeat themselves.

"But that's not how we act. That's not how we treat people. That's not what our church is like."

Whether you like it or not, in the minds of anyone who has ever had an experience with any church—whether positive or negative—*your* church is marked by all their previous experiences with churches. Not only is this a reality, it is also a reasonable reality. We develop an understanding of the world based upon the experiences that we've had. To expect someone to just forget or overlook previous experiences with a church simply because we've assured them that "we're not like that" is to ask them to act in a way that is contrary to the way we ourselves act in every avenue of life.

The criticisms are fair if they are accurate reflections of previous experiences. We know that the church has caused harm to people, therefore the criticisms are fair.

This is not to say that every story of church hurt is true or that we, as a church, should not seek the Holy Spirit's guidance in discerning the truth and what our response should be. It is simply to say that the evidence backs up the truth of many of these claims and, as such, we need to acknowledge the claims and lead with belief rather than skepticism.

Most of this chapter, thus far, has been focused on generic criticisms of the generic church and how the church, broadly speaking, should reflect on them. As we just established, a criticism against one church is—in essence—a criticism against all churches because we are all one body in Christ and because one's experience in any church is taken as a representative experience of all churches. But what about your church specifically?

We've shied away from that question so far because we want to be sure that we acknowledge the ways in which we are culpable in the minds of those who have been harmed by the church. And yet, each church—as an individual representation of the body of Christ—bears responsibility to every church and to Christ himself for the way it lives out that representation. So, in one sense we are inextricably *linked* to the behavior of all churches but we are only directly *responsible* for our own.

In Rev 2–3, the words of Jesus come to the seven churches (Ephesus, Smyrna, Pergamum, Thyatira, Sardis, Philadelphia, and Laodicea). Each church receives a unique, personalized word from Jesus concerning its work, its condition, its level of faithfulness, and so on. These words are often a combination of commendation and correction and challenge.

For instance, to the church in Ephesus Jesus says, "I know you are enduring patiently and bearing up for my name's sake, and you have not grown weary. But I have this against you, that you have abandoned the love you had at first. Remember therefore from where you have fallen; repent and do the works you did at first" (Rev 2:3–5a).

In these two and a half verses Jesus commends their endurance, corrects their failure to hold fast to him, and challenges them to repent.

In another instance, to the church in Thyatira Jesus says, "I know your works, your love and faith and service and patient endurance and that your latter works exceed the first. But I have this against you, that you tolerate that woman Jezebel, who calls herself a prophetess and is teaching and seducing my servants to practice sexual immorality and to eat food sacrificed to idols." Then, skipping to verse 24: "But to the rest of you in Thyatira, who do not hold this teaching, who have not learned what some call the deep things of Satan, to you I say, I do not lay on you any other burden. Only hold fast what you have until I come" (Rev 2:19–20, 24–25).

In these four verses Jesus commends their work, corrects their sexual impurity, and challenges them to hold on to his teachings.

Jesus gives a unique, specific message to each church, holding them accountable, not for what the other churches have done, but for the things that he taught them. He examines each church in light of his commands and his expectations and he outlines for each church exactly where they have fallen short. In doing this he doesn't offer condemnation (Rom 8:1), but he offers correction and a reminder that failure to hold to the faith—failure to hold on

INSIDE-OUT

to him and his commands—is to turn their backs on him. Jesus tells the church in Ephesus that failure to hear and heed his warnings will result in him coming to remove the lampstand—that is, to remove his light—from its place.

Zooming in, then, from an examination of the church as a whole to your individual church, the question to consider is what is the fruit of your church's work? This can be seen in the many integrated facets of your church, from leadership to membership to discipleship to mission to commitment to accountability and response to correction. The fruit follows the functioning.

LEADERSHIP

Do those in leadership in your church have healthy home lives (1 Tim 3:4-5)? Are they leading from a position of integrity (Matt 23:2-3)? Do they seek opportunities to serve both the congregation and the community (Matt 20:25-28)? Are they quick to listen and slow to speak (Jas 1:19)? Do they build up the church (Eph 4:29)?

Many of these questions and scriptures apply to all who are in the church, but these are especially necessary for those in leadership. It is undesirable that any in the church habitually fail in any of these questions, but it is *unacceptable* that any in leadership habitually fail in any of these questions.

MEMBERSHIP

Does the membership of your church respect those in leadership, following their guidance, relying on their counsel, and submit to their authority (Heb 13:17)? Do they look forward to and enjoy worshiping and fellowshiping together *and* do they do it even when it feels like a burden (Acts 2:42 and Heb 10:24-25)? Are they supportive and loving of each other when there are difficulties and arguments (Phil 2:1-4)?

DISCIPLESHIP

Does your church have an understanding of what discipleship is and how it works? Is discipleship modeled by leadership in their relationships with the members? Does your church hold discipleship in high regard, challenging young and old, rookie and veteran alike in growing in their faith?

MISSION

Does your church have a clear mission that is clearly understood by the membership? Is your mission centered on the tenets of the Great Commission? Does your church regularly reconsider its mission as well as its overall effectiveness in meeting the expectations of the mission?

COMMITMENT

Do most of your members attend most of your meetings most of the time? Do most of your members participate in most of your outreach and evangelism activities most of the time? Is it apparent in the lives of your membership that they have bought into the mission of the church and that they look for opportunities to participate in that mission on a weekly basis?

A softer approach to the questions of commitment might seem necessary, especially acknowledging the changing culture and the different ways in which people have come to interact with the church in the grand scheme of their lives. It is true that the life of the church is no longer the central feature it used to be in the family and in the community. Yet while this is the case, our commitment to Christ and his mission remains ever-necessary and the church remains the primary institution dedicated to fulfilling this mission. Since this aspect of the church and its expected work remains, there is no room to soften these questions on commitment. Even as the ways in which the church works have shifted, there is no shift in Jesus' expectation that we be committed members of it.

ACCOUNTABILITY AND RESPONSE TO CORRECTION

What is your reaction when presented with thoughtful correction from fellow members? What is your reaction when presented with thoughtful criticism from people outside the church? When confronted with Scripture that challenges the way you think, believe, or act, are you softened by the work of the Spirit or are you hardened by the work of your flesh?

All of these things—leadership, membership, discipleship, mission, commitment, and accountability—are the raw materials your church has at its disposal for producing fruit for the kingdom. Weakness in any of these areas diminishes the quality of the work you do and the outcome of the work you do.

What remains the same, no matter whether you have great strengths or great weaknesses or some combination, is that the results of your work is always your fruit.

Countless children, women, and men fed every week by your church's food pantry? That is the fruit of your church.

Six middle-school kids come to saving faith in Jesus during your church's vacation Bible school program? That is the fruit of your church.

One single mother who lost her job and is in need of money for utilities is turned away? That is the fruit of your church.

Twenty-seven kids go from newborn through high school in your congregation and only two of them remain faithful followers of Jesus? That is the fruit of your church.

No matter the outcomes, each church is responsible to Jesus for the people it encounters, the gifts is has, and how faithful it is. This is not a time for shame or for guilt; rather it is a time for reflection, conviction, and repentance. The fruit that your church has produced to this point is the reality you must face. That can't be changed. What can be changed, however, is what your church does now.

The call to unearth the church should begin to hit home now.

Unearth the Church

When the church is inwardly focused—thinking primarily about itself—the reason it does what it does is pretty straightforward: "We do this in this way because it supports this thing that the we enjoy and value." But when the church becomes outwardly focused—mirroring the commissioning of Jesus—the reasons it does things change as do the things it does.

This means that there are things—activities, practices, attitudes—that the church currently holds onto that will need to be let go of. This means that there are things that your church has done for many years that will need to be adjusted or jettisoned.

A couple times a year my wife steps into our garage and determines that it is time to clean. So, we begin by removing everything from the garage and placing it on the driveway. After that we sweep out all of the dirt and rocks and leaves that have been carried in over the previous six months. Once the garage floor is cleaned as well as a garage floor can be cleaned, we begin the process of assessing everything that we took out of the garage.

We're often shocked at this point, wondering how it is possible that all of that stuff fit in the garage in the first place. After the shock wears off, we start making piles: one pile to be kept, one pile to be trashed, and one pile to be discussed further. After everything has been assigned to a pile we start carrying things to the trash, putting things back in the garage, and discussing what to do with the stuff in the remaining pile.

Then, when everything is swept, sorted, and set back in place we stand in the garage and consider how much nicer it looks and how good it is to have that job done.

This is the central work—the primary effort—of unearthing the church. Before any other steps can be taken, we first have to be willing to acknowledge that things aren't quite how they should be. Indeed, how *could* things be how they should be when we haven't yet been perfected? When we acknowledge that not everything is in order, we start by putting everything out on the driveway, exposing it to the light of day. We turn back to Christ as our foundation, sweeping away any remnants of the way we were before we turned to him, and starting again with that foundation, we reconsider each and every thing that is on the driveway.

We consider each principle, each thought, each practice, holding each up against the backdrop of Scripture, asking the Holy Spirit to help us discern which things are good and which things are garbage, which things we put back on the foundation, and which things we cast aside. As we go through this inside-out evaluation, what becomes clear is that if there is anything that we are not willing to put out on the driveway for reconsideration, then we aren't really ready and willing to be used in the way that Jesus commands us to be.

To paraphrase the words of Jesus, "If anyone would come after me, let him [empty out his garage] and take up his cross and follow me. For whoever would save his life will lose it, but whoever loses his life for my sake will find it" (Matt 16:24–25).

POST SCRIPTS

PS to the Non-Church

As far as universally applicable practices go, this cleaning-out-the-garage practice ranks pretty high on the list. Whether you have any inclination toward Christianity and toward the church or not, reorienting toward your desired goals and eliminating things that are hindering your progress toward your desired goals just makes sense in the grand scheme of life (that is, assuming that your goals are beneficial and worthwhile).

I find myself wondering, at this point, what kinds of things might be coming to mind for you as you think about cleaning out your own garage. What habits or thoughts do you carry around that are weighing you down? This is not an attempt to take the focus off of the work that the church needs to do; however, there is truth to the idea that none of us—no individual or organization—is doing everything exactly right. If that's the case, then I'm sure there are things that you might be struggling with, wondering if it is time to let those things go.

Whatever those things are, my prayer is that you will be given clarity, that you will be able to face them down, and that you will find a new path forward.

PS to the Church

I don't know how much of a notetaker or a margin-writer you are, but if you have any tendency toward those actions, here is your call to action.

I am confident that there are some things that came to mind for you as you were reading about cleaning out the garage. I am confident that there are things that you've been struggling with in your church and in your life, things that you know are preventing you and your church from being as effective as could be. I am also confident that there are things that have come to mind that you do not want to acknowledge yet; things that you think are probably just fine, but *may* not be.

Jot those things down. Write them in the margins, on a sticky note, send yourself a text, whatever you need to do, just get them jotted down.

Once you've done that, pray about those things regularly. Ask God to show you clearly which are things that need to be jettisoned and, as God makes that clear to you, jettison them.

There is nothing in your life—individually or corporately—that is worth holding onto if, in holding onto it, you harm the church, its witness, or the people the church is called to witness to.

6

Belief, Action, Fruit

ONE OF THE DANGERS in considering the fruit of our actions—that is, the results of our actions—is that it can be tempting to fall into the the-end-justifies-the-means mentality. "As long as the outcome is desirable," the thinking goes, "the method and process of getting there is immaterial."

This is an ethic that most if not all of us would reject on its face.

For example, you may want to buy a new video game console for your children for Christmas. Okay, that's fine. There's likely no harm in doing that. However, if you have to trample over another person in the midst of a mad scramble during a Black Friday sale in order to get the video game console, then there is harm.

This consideration can be—and has been—taken into far more serious, far more existential hypotheticals and real-world scenarios. Whether its family relationships or matters of governance or the ethics of wartime tactics, the question that overhangs the situation is this: at what point does the harm caused by the means outweigh the benefit of the outcome?

To bring this clearly back into the realm of the church, consider this statement: "I will do anything short of sinning to reach people for Jesus." This has become a common mantra among many pastors. At first glance it may seem like an okay statement. Someone may think, "I mean, they said they aren't going to sin, but they'll do anything else. That sounds like they're committed and are willing to go to great lengths for the gospel and for the people who haven't heard it."

One of the principles of the Christian life is that a Christian should be above reproach. This is especially true for those in positions of Christian leadership (Titus 1:7 and 1 Tim 3:2), but it is also true for Christians no matter what their rank or station. Christians have been reconciled to God—brought back into relationship with God—by the work of Jesus and this allows Christians to be presented to God as "holy and blameless and above reproach" (Col 1:21–23).

It's not enough, though, simply to be above reproach. Scripture also commands Christians to "abstain from every form of evil" (1 Thess 5:22). Or, as the old King James Version puts it, "Abstain from all appearance of evil."

Taking this one step further, 2 Tim 2:15 tells Christians the following: "Do your best to present yourself to God as one approved, a worker who has no need to be ashamed, rightly handling the word of truth."

So Christians must be above reproach, avoid all forms of evil—even the appearance of evil—and strive to present themselves before God in a way that he would approve. Do you see how the bar set by "anything short of sin" transgresses the standard that Scripture puts in place? God is the arbiter of that standard—that line—and Scripture again and again challenges and commands Christians to completely steer clear of that line, not to tiptoe up to it and come up with a cute slogan to use as a justification for borderline behavior.

There are certain actions that are inexcusable no matter what outcome the actions might produce.

So, while the fruit of our actions is important, the fruit itself does not point to right belief and right action. The fruit cannot be used as a smokescreen or as an excuse for sin or for harm that happens behind the scenes. It is as glaring a warning sign as there

BELIEF, ACTION, FRUIT

can be when someone's sin is exposed and they immediately point to their fruit.

Good fruit is not an excuse for sin. Good fruit that comes from a sinful situation is not an exoneration of sin; rather, it is evidence that God can use anyone at anytime in any circumstance to bring about good (Gen 50:18–20).

Our desire, as followers of Jesus, should be to be used by God for his purposes and that we would be in line with his will every step of the way, from belief to action to fruit. This is the trajectory that we will follow in this chapter as we consider the church in light of the outside-in assessment, the inside-out assessment, and the commands of Scripture.

What do we believe, how do we act as a result of that belief, and what is the expected fruit of that action?

Let's return the story of Jesus driving the money changers out of the temple grounds. He chases them out telling them that they have turned God's house into a house of robbers and thieves.

They were robbing the people of their money by charging exorbitant prices.

They were robbing the people of their access to the house of the Lord.

They were robbing God of glory and worship by placing themselves in between him and the people.

These men were thieves at least three times over.

No matter what these merchants and money changers believed to be true about God, it is clear that they also believed it was okay—good, even—for them to be placing themselves in the space between God and the people. They believed that it was okay for them to exact a profit from the spiritual act of sacrifice. They believed they were in the right according to precedent and tradition.

How can we know that this is what they believed? Because their actions betray their beliefs. If they had believed that the temple was primarily a place of sacrifice, worship, and fellowship among people of like minds and with a like faith, they would have—in the very least—conducted their business in the marketplace rather than on the temple grounds. But their actions demonstrate that this is not what they believed. No, they believed in profit and their actions were aimed at profit.

The fruit of their actions based upon the testimony of Scripture is at least fourfold:

1. The disenfranchisement of the poor was their fruit.
2. The undermining of the dignity of the temple grounds was their fruit.
3. The upholding of tradition over and above the law and love of God was their fruit.
4. The lining of their pockets was their fruit.

When Jesus entered that scene—Jesus who knows the thoughts and intentions of the heart—he didn't see men who were providing a necessary service or men whose work was focused on glorifying God. No, he saw greedy men who wanted to convert God's commands and glory into profit for themselves.

They believed in profit. They exploited the sacrificial system. They enriched themselves.

Belief. Action. Fruit.

Surely there is a one-to-one comparison to be made between this story and some people in some churches. Most, if not all, preachers who fall in the "prosperity gospel" camp come to mind. Throughout the history of religion, whether Eastern or Western, there have been religious people who have been willing to stoop to great depths to enrich themselves off of the devotion and vulnerability of the faithful.

This points us again to the importance of right belief.

Clearly, Jesus is the apex example of right belief, action, and fruit. Clearly, the money changers and merchants on the temple grounds fell far short of that example. Jesus was exactly right and the merchants were exactly wrong.

There is a wide gap between the two examples.

Where do you fall on that continuum?

I stated in chapter 2 that Jesus' vision, expectation, and command to his followers is that they would minister in a way that is consistent with his ministry and they would do this all over the world by the power of the Holy Spirit. This vision that Jesus laid out for his church was to be put into effect by believers' obedience to the Great Commission.

Jesus' vision for his church has been entrusted to believers. What we believe—how closely we adhere to the teachings of Jesus—is critical to the success of the mission.

It is important for the church to think about the ways in which it has been successful and the times it has made great strides for the kingdom. But, it is also important—I'd suggest even more important—for the church to think about the ways in which it has failed and the times it has created setbacks or stumbling blocks for the kingdom and for those who might become members of it. This fruit points to wrong belief and, in turn, to wrong action.

This is not to say that an unsuccessful outreach event is a sign of wrong belief and action. It might be, but that is not the focus here. This is also not to say that dwindling membership and attendance is a sign of wrong belief and action. It might be, but that is not the focus here. The focus here is on the people the church is called to serve in the name of Jesus.

Go back once again to the clearing of the temple. Jesus has driven out those who were taking advantage of religious devotion and abusing the people they should have been serving. Then, when the coast was clear, the people who had been kept at a distance for one reason or another—people who found themselves on the outskirts—"came to him in the temple, and he healed them" (Matt 21:14).

Christian, do you—as you sit there right now—still believe that you need Jesus? Do you recognize your deep need for his mercy, grace, forgiveness, and love? Are you just as overwhelmed by the gift of salvation today as you were when you first received it?

When I started seminary, I started with the notion that I was going to become an expert in the Bible and in theology. I would spend my years in study and I would come out on the other side fully informed, armed with all the answers to all the questions that anyone might ask.

Whether it is seminary or any other specialty, anyone who has dived into the depths of learning eventually realizes just how naive that notion I had when I entered seminary was. The more focused on an area of study you become, the more aware you become of how little you know. No matter how long you study and learn, the distance between how much you know and how much you know you don't know only gets wider. Yes, you learn and grow, but you never know it all.

Proximity illuminates depths and details that are unseeable from a distance.

Keeping our eyes on Jesus serves a twofold purpose: first, it keeps us aligned in our walk as followers and, second, it reminds us of just how far from perfection we are. The closer we follow after Jesus, the more aware we are of how far we fall short. The closer we follow after Jesus, the more convicted we are of our ongoing sinfulness. The closer we follow after Jesus, the more passion we have to bring the gospel to those who do not have it.

The "Christian judgmentalism" that motivates some of us to hold people at a distance from Jesus and from his church is not exhibited by those who walk closely to Jesus; rather, it is exhibited by people who have either forgotten or never knew how much they need him. To act that way is to guard the temple grounds just like the merchants. We like to think that we would have been standing right there with Jesus, whip in hand, helping him clear out the temple. But the odds are that if we weren't among the blind and the lame—among the ones who came to Jesus knowing just how much they needed him—we likely would have been among the people Jesus drove out.

If we are to minister in a way that is consistent with the ministry of Jesus and hold to the expectations of the Great Commission, then we need to grow in our Christlikeness, not in our religiosity—religiosity is what the people Jesus drove out of the temple grounds were good at. If we want to be effective ministers of the gospel and if we want our churches to be welcoming and effective outposts for the kingdom, then we need to be humble in our assessment of everything that we believe and do—in all matters of faith and practice.

What is the recent fruit of your church?

How is that fruit a reflection of the actions you have taken?

How are those actions a reflection of your beliefs?

Are those beliefs in line with the ministry and teachings of Jesus?

When working on the assessment of fruit, be careful not to be too results focused. Part of the fruit of your church will be seen in the results of evangelistic outreach and in how the community surrounding your church perceives your church, but part of the fruit of your church will be seen in the attitudes and discipleship trends amongst your membership.

I have been part of enough churches in my lifetime and heard enough stories in my lifetime to know that the attitudes of the members and their commitment-level to discipleship are the first fruits that need to be considered. Interestingly, there is a directly-proportional relationship between commitment to discipleship and overall attitudes. As the church's commitment to discipleship increases, the attitudes of the membership improve. As the church's commitment to discipleship decreases, the attitudes of the membership get worse.

If there is disagreement without resolution, anger without conversation, seemingly unprovoked attacks, passive-aggressiveness, negativity without constructive observations, or any other such unproductive interactions going on in your church, it is likely that the commitment to discipleship is in need of attention.

Discipleship is the process by which mature believers nurture young believers into Christlikeness through instruction, encouragement, accountability, conversation, and prayer. Discipleship is the process through which the old self is done away with and the new self is nurtured. Discipleship is the process by which those who are justified—those who have been made right with God by the work of Jesus—are then sanctified—are moved away from sinfulness and toward righteousness.

It is a little on the nose perhaps, but discipleship is what Jesus has in mind in the Great Commission when he says, "Go therefore and make *disciples* of all nations, baptizing them in the name of the Father and of the Son and of the Holy Spirit, teaching them to observe all that I have commanded you" (Matt 28:19–20a).

A culture of discipleship and the ongoing work of discipleship and the maturing of disciples is the most important and most telling fruit of a church. Doing this work and developing this culture is the command Jesus gave to his church in the post-resurrection world.

How is your church doing with discipleship?

What is your members' attitudes toward each other and toward those in the community?

If discipleship is not the primary fruit of your church, the following statements are likely true about your church:

1. Your beliefs are not scripturally aligned.

2. You don't understand your calling.

3. You are serving the money changers to the exclusion of the blind and lame.

4. You are not helping your community.

If discipleship is not the primary fruit of your church, what are the things that are getting in the way, the things that are standing between you and the call of Christ in the Great Commission? It is likely impossible to create an exhaustive list in response to that question, but here are a few things to consider:

EVERYTHING'S FINE

Why in the world would anyone change anything when everything is fine exactly as it is? This question—though a bit tongue-in-cheek—is at the heart of the "everything's fine" obstacle. A church—especially a long-lived church—is great at pretending that there aren't any problems. This is seen in shallow, event-focused conversations. This is seen in a lack of intimacy. This is seen in weak commitment levels. Everyone pretends that everything is fine because if anyone admits that anything is wrong, the charade parade comes to an end and people have to decide to work or run. It's no fun if work is involved, so let's just keep on pretending.

REMEMBER WHEN?

Some in the church have become willing to admit that things aren't great. But, this admission comes at a price—you have to offer an alternative vision if you're going to bring up a failing. Rather than consider growth—which would require reprioritization and work—they opt for gazing into the past at a time when things were better.

"Yep, the only reason things aren't great now is because we aren't doing things the way we used to. Remember when we had that program? Remember when the pews were full of children? Remember when that pastor was here? Oh his sermons were so inspiring an motivating."

CONFLICT

This one is less of a crutch and more of an illness. Churches that are infected with the illness of conflict are so busy focusing on themselves and their anger that they simply can't focus on doing Great Commission work. Some churches relish conflict, though they'd never admit it. Some churches create conflict because they don't know how to communicate or relate in any other way.

Don't forget that churches are made up of people and that people have personal histories that they bring with them into all areas of their lives. I am not a psychologist, so I will not attempt to delve into the psychology; I will, however, say that when people become accustomed to communicating and relating in a certain way, it takes a lot to change.

A church that is not committed to discipleship has no reason to expect the conflict will ever be resolved. It doesn't matter if the conflict came in with a new member or if the conflict has long-existed in the church, resolution is not in sight. So, rather than resolving anything, this church often becomes an "everything's fine" church instead.

LESS ACTION MORE TALK

In this church, people are pretty good about identifying the problems that are facing the church. In this church, people are even good at understanding that a lack of discipleship or poor attitudes may be the main culprit. But, in this church, people are so good at talking about these things—setting meetings and strategizing and developing action items and considering all the pros and cons—that they never get around to doing anything about the problems they've identified. For these churches, the committees and task forces themselves are sufficient. As long as they see it and talk about it, they're good.

Wrestling with the ways in which our beliefs, actions, and fruit do not line up with the teachings, commands, and expectations of Jesus is critical to the process of unearthing the church. The above obstacles—along with many others—often serve as the church's desired buffer; the identifiable and acceptable things that stand between us and the work Jesus calls us to. Failing to identify and unearth these things is to fail the entirety of the unearthing process.

It is true that it is easier to say everything's fine or to harken back to day's long past or to languish in conflict or to just talk a good game than it is to undertake the grueling task of putting everything out on the driveway, asking God to tell us what we should keep and what we should chuck. It is easier, for sure, but if you're anything like me you're sick of that game and you're ready to try Jesus' plan instead.

If you believe in Jesus, you must follow his commands. If you follow his commands, the fruit of your effort will benefit your church and your community.

We can only get to this point, though, if we stand on the right foundation.

POST SCRIPTS

PS to the Non-Church

As you reflect on your experience with the church and its members, has it been your experience that this "belief, action, fruit" continuum has been out of balance? Has your experience with the church and its members been marked more by judgment/condemnation or more by empathy? Do you feel like the church and its members should be better at living like Jesus themselves before they try to make you into a disciple too?

It is an all too easy escape hatch from accountability for some random Christian in some random church to look at you and say, "Look, all of your negative experiences with the church are because you've never experienced what the church is supposed to be like—you should try *my* church." The sentiment behind that statement is true, but an adjacent truth is this: as long as the church is made up of human-beings, the church is never going to live up to the standard Jesus set for it.

So this is an acknowledgment of your experience; the "belief, action, fruit" continuum in the church has been out of balance. We have held up ourselves as the standard all the while failing to live up to the standard that Jesus set. This book, then, is an attempt to redirect attention—both the church's and yours—back to Jesus and, in the process, start to shake off all of the bits and pieces that have thrown the church's balance off.

PS to the Church

Again and again, as I contemplate the church and where we are, I come upon a moment when I think, "Is it just me? Am I the only one who has seen or experienced this in the church?" Then I read another article or have another conversation and I see, once again, just how common these experiences are. In this chapter, this "is it just me" thought came to mind in thinking about the things that stand in between the church and the work of the Great Commission: everything's fine, remember when, conflict, less action more talk.

Is it just me?

The struggle that we face in the church is often much less about knowing what the right beliefs, actions, and fruits are and much more often about these obstacles that we erect between the way we normally function and the way we ought to function. This is a common organizational truth—whether the church or any other organization that is made up of people—and this truth reveals that we are more concerned with precedent and comfort than we are with what is good and right.

It's not just me. I'm sure you feel it too.

Be careful here church. Condemnation lies in the wake of thwarted conviction. You will not save yourself by doing good things—salvation comes only through faith in Jesus—but you may very well condemn yourself by not doing the good that you know you should.

7

The Foundation

WHAT IS THE CHURCH'S foundation? Where and upon what do we stand? At this point in the unearthing process we have arrived at the foundation level and need to take a look around to assess exactly where we are. As you consider the unearthed landscape around you, what do you see? What don't you see?

If everything seems okay to you—like your life and your church and your community are right where you think they should be—then I'd challenge you to look again, not from the perspective of what you want but from the perspective of what Jesus commands.

Consider again Jesus' challenge to the church in Ephesus.

> I know you are enduring patiently and bearing up for my name's sake, and you have not grown weary. But I have this against you, that you have abandoned the love you had at first. Repent therefore from where you have fallen; repent, and do the works you did at first. If not, I will come to you and remove your lampstand from its place, unless you repent. (Rev 2:3-5)

Jesus' words to the church in Ephesus are to a group of people who likely looked at their church and their work and their lives and their communities and felt that things were in order. But

Jesus looked at them in all of those things and he saw that they had fallen away from their first love, their commitment to him, and their desire to grow in faith and in grace. They had adopted a therapeutic spirituality in which they were sustained by the principles of Christianity and not by Jesus himself.

Christianity is not founded on principles and the church is not founded on ideas. Both Christianity and the church are founded on Jesus; on his life, death, resurrection, and commands. Jesus did not come and live and die and defeat sin and death and hell so that we could have comfortable church communities, sheltered from the difficulties of the world. The mark of a Christian or of a church in pursuit of Jesus is not the absence of struggles. Far from it. The mark of a Christian and of a church in pursuit of Jesus is endurance in the face of struggles.

This point is addressed again and again in the Scriptures in the words of Jesus and the apostles. Here are just a few examples:

In John 16:33 Jesus said to the disciples, "In the world you will have tribulation."

In Matt 5:11, as Jesus is presenting the Sermon on the Mount, he said, "Blessed are you when others revile you and persecute you and utter all kinds of evil against you falsely on my account."

In John 15:19, Jesus tells the disciples, "If you were of the world, the world would love you as its own; but because you are not of the world, but I chose you out of the world, therefore the world hates you."

Paul, in his letter to the churches of Rome, wrote, "The Spirit himself bears witness with our spirit that we are children of God, and if children, then heirs—heirs of God and fellow heirs with Christ, provided we suffer with him in order that we may also be glorified with him" (Rom 8:16–17).

Or, as Paul wrote to Timothy, "Indeed, all who desire to live a godly life in Christ Jesus will be persecuted" (2 Tim 3:12).

And, as a final example, Peter wrote, "Beloved, do not be surprised at the fiery trial when it comes upon you to test you, as though something strange were happening to you. But rejoice

THE FOUNDATION

insofar as you share in Christ's sufferings, that you may also rejoice and be glad when his glory is revealed" (1 Pet 4:12–13).

Additionally, the constancy—even the necessity—of struggle is a point that is seen again and again in nearly every scriptural narrative. A quick recap of the lives of Abraham, Joseph, Moses, Ruth, and Paul reveals the theme of personal struggle, hardship, faith, and perseverance.

As we established a moment ago, the mark of a Christian and of a church in pursuit of Jesus is endurance in the face of struggles, not the absence of struggles. So, if as you assess where you and your church are at this point and you feel that you are okay—that everything's fine—just take a moment to consider the possibility that you are missing something. More forcefully, if you assess that you and your church are just fine, then it is almost certain that you are missing something and that you need to lift up some rugs and peak behind some curtains; you yet have unearthing to do.

There is always room for growth and maturity in ourselves and in our churches and failure to see it only means that we've got some blind spots. We all have blind spots. This is why the unearthing process is necessary; over time each of us becomes blind to the fact that we created many of the religious structures that exist around us in order to serve our preferences rather than the ministry of Jesus. To go another step—and what makes many of these things so hard to see and so insidious—is that we often conflate our preferences with the ministry of Jesus. So, we often can't see or understand how something that we've always done is harming our ability to minister.

Assessing what the foundation is, then, requires a diagnostic process. It requires a way for us to objectively assess the lay of the land at the foundation level. It requires prayer, reflection, honesty, and action.

PRAYER

Dear God, we want to be up front with you. Sometimes we think that the way we are living and the way we are running the church is just right. Sometimes we think that the only problem the church has is that not enough people listen to our ideas because we think we've got it figured out. Other times, God, we get stuck in a place thinking that nothing's right, that nothing ever will be right, and that we'd be better off just quitting. At this point, we admit that both of those ideas are lies. We know that we don't have it figured out and we also know that there is reason to hope. Help us, O God, to remember that you *do* have it figured out and that you are the reason we have to hope. Help us, O God, to not shy away from the truths you would have us see. Help us, O God, to repent of excuses and lies and false foundations. Help us, O God, to stop relying on our own understanding and, instead, to rely on your revelation and truth. Guide us, challenge us, stretch us, and comfort us. Amen.

REFLECTION

Reflection is not an easy task. When you think about reflection, you may have a few ideas come to mind. Maybe you think about simply looking at how things are. Maybe you think about remembering or reminiscing. Reflection—as it is being used here—is not really any of those things. Instead, it is a challenge to look critically at where you are right now and to consider how you got here; to consider what beliefs, decisions, and actions have led you to this place. Reflection, in this sense, is a challenge to look at your foundation.

There is personal utility to this exercise, but for the purposes of unearthing the church, we're going to keep this at a corporate level; that is, at a church level. First, I'm going to provide some reflection questions/prompts that will be helpful for you to consider and then I will lay out a hypothetical example in which these reaction questions/prompts have been considered.

1. Identify—Identify something (program, ministry, relationship, etc.) in your church that is not working as intended.
2. Stated Goal—What is the stated goal of that program?

3. Shortfalls—What are the ways in which the real outcome does not match the stated goal?

4. Motivation—What does the real outcome reveal about the motivation behind the program and/or the people involved?

5. Foundation—What does this suggest about the foundational principles of the church?

Here is an example of the application of these questions/prompts in evaluation of a church program:

1. Identify—Youth outreach program

2. Stated Goal—Adults in the church will establish connections with youth in the Community by mentoring, discipling, and encouraging them

3. Shortfalls—Youth in the community are not responsive to invitations; adults in the church—disappointed by the lack of response—no longer not show up on time or at all; despite a couple of early connections in the community those connections have fizzled and the only youth connected to the program now are the ones who were in the church to begin with; people in the church seem content to say, "At least we tried"

4. Motivation—Growth, immediate success, a confusion between activity and ministry, and catharsis

5. Foundation—Based upon this example, the foundational principles of the church as seen in this failing youth outreach program are obligation, entitlement, and laziness.

In the 1989 movie *Field of Dreams* (apologies for any spoilers), a farmer named Ray hears a voice that says, "If you build it, he will come."[1] In watching the movie you discover that the "it" Ray builds is a baseball diamond and the "he" who comes to the field is the ghost of Ray's father.

This quote from *Field of Dreams* is often misquoted as "if you build it, they will come" and this misquotation has been adopted

1. Robinson, *Field of Dreams*.

as a truism of sorts. I remember being part of a church in the early nineties that was considering a building project to expand its facilities. My father—who was pastor of that church and, as it turns out, a fan of that movie—would occasionally quote that line as part of his rhetorical defense for undertaking the building project. "If we want people to show up at our church," the thinking went, "then we need to build a place that will accommodate them when they show up."

Is it wrong to undertake building projects and to develop new programming initiatives? Not necessarily, but we've got to remember the belief, action, fruit paradigm.

Many churches, whether aware of it or not, adopt this "if you build it" mentality when it comes to buildings and programs, thinking that the only barrier standing in the way of growth is building a thing—a structure, a program, a brand. So, focused on growth and the prospect of success, the church undertakes the construction of whatever it is they believe will make it so that people will come.

Hopefully the error here is clear. To focus on growth is to neglect health. A church that sets its eyes on growth is a church that has taken its eyes off of Jesus. A church that aims for growth instead of health will find neither. A church that is motivated by growth may increase in size—indeed, many churches with this motivation have done exactly that—but these churches are serving the outcome, not the Savior.

There are any number of things that a church can do over the course of its existence in the service of Jesus. Whether it is a youth outreach program or community evangelism or a food pantry or small group book studies, if it is done with the express hope of numerical growth, it is done for the wrong reason. It is critical to remember that if we place our focus on growth, we will miss the same thing the merchants and money changers on the temple grounds missed: the people we are called to love, serve, and lead to Jesus.

THE FOUNDATION

HONESTY

There are two temptations to be avoided at this foundational level. The first is the temptation to create a problem where there is no problem. The second is to sugar-coat reality. There is a needle that must be threaded in order to get between those two temptations when it comes to honesty about our foundations. In the first case, it may be tempting to just invent a problem while, in the second case, it may be tempting to just not look very closely so as not to see the problems that are there.

What is the church's foundation? Where and upon what do we stand? As you consider the unearthed landscape around you, what do you see? What don't you see?

In the example above—the failing youth outreach program—the foundational principles at play in that church were obligation, entitlement, and laziness.

Does the quick start followed by a quick fizzle of that program resonate with your experience? Do you find that excitement exists in the planning but pessimism exists in the execution. Are you disappointed by limited and shrinking participation in programming initiatives? Do you wonder at your own commitment, trying to understand why you just don't want to keep trying?

When the church undertakes any activity—whether worship or outreach, fellowship or evangelism—simply because they feel like they have to do it or because these are the sort of things that churches do, the foundational principle of the church in those activities is obligation. Can God bless the things that we do out of obligation? Yes (and its a good thing because so much of what the church does falls under this heading). However, our call in Jesus is not to do things because we have to but, rather, to do things because we love him (1 John 5:1–3).

When the church's activities meet roadblocks and failure and the members resort to blame and finger-pointing as they wonder out loud, "What was the point of it all?" the foundational principle of the church in those activities is entitlement.

When the church gives up because of adverse results, the foundational principle of the church in those activities is laziness.

Again, do any of these situations and attitudes resonate with you and your experience in the church? I'm sure they do. And I'm sure, if you're being honest with yourself, that these situations and attitudes resonate with your experience of yourself at times as well.

What each of these foundational principles shares in common is a focus on self and a rejection of Jesus. Obligation is selfish in that we only do things so that people won't bother us for not doing them. Entitlement is selfish, obviously, because we're focused on getting what we think we deserve. Laziness is selfish in that the only effort it requires is that which we already feel like doing.

There are any number of foundational principles that might pop up in our own real-world evaluation of our experience of the church or of ourselves within the church. Any given experience, when evaluated, might reveal something new about the foundation of your church, helping to shine the light on all of the various facets of the selfishness that has taken the place of Jesus.

When words like "obligated" and "entitled" and "lazy" and "selfish" start getting tossed around, another word often get tossed in the mix as well: defensive. Are you feeling accused? Are you feeling defensive? Are you thinking, "Sure, things aren't exactly how I'd like them to be in my church, but we're not entitled and lazy"?

There are traps at these depths; traps that serve the purpose of undermining the possibility of conviction, confession, repentance, and sanctification to yield their intended fruit. The most likely trap you'll encounter is right in front of you right now. It is the holier-than-thou trap and you need to watch your step.

In Luke 18, Jesus shares a parable about "two men who went into the temple to pray, one a Pharisee and the other a tax collector" (Luke 18:10). In that culture, the Pharisee was seen as a holy man whose actions were to be admired and followed and, conversely, the tax collector was seen as a greedy man who had betrayed his people and was deserving of God's wrath. Jesus shares what each of these man prayed.

THE FOUNDATION

The Pharisee spoke to God, saying, "'God, I thank you that I am not like other men, extortioners, unjust, adulterers, or even like this tax collector.' . . . But the tax collector, standing far off, would not even lift up his eyes to heaven, but beat his breast, saying, 'God, be merciful to me, a sinner!'" (Luke 18:11, 13).

Jesus concludes this parable about the Pharisee and the tax collector this way: "I tell you, [the tax collector] went down to his house justified, rather than the [Pharisee]. For everyone who exalts himself will be humbled, but the one who humbles himself will be exalted" (Luke 18:10–14).

The point of comparison that matters here is how unfavorably we measure up to Jesus and his commands, not how favorably we might match up to some other person or some other church. If that Pharisee's foundation and focus was on God rather than on himself and the people he was so sure he was better than, his self-assessment would have been the same as the tax collector's.

Is it possible that there is no part of your church's membership and ministry that is founded on Jesus? Sure, it is possible, though not likely. The more important factor here is that no matter how good things may be in your church's life and ministry, there are certainly things that are founded on something *other* than Jesus.

The hard truth of the matter is that the sicker you are the harder it will be for you to see it. Why? Because you've grown unaccustomed to the voice and likeness of Jesus. Because you've walked away from the mirror of his word and have forgotten what he looks like and, by extension, what you are supposed to look like. Because you can't remember what a healthy church looks like.

When the fruit of the church is conflict, stagnant congregations, and millions of disaffected or injured former members it is clear that the foundation we hoped to have discovered underneath it all isn't what we've actually unearthed. Stumbling around on a foundation of selfishness will never lead to health or sacrificial service, only to greater conflict and stagnation, more and more disaffected and injured former members, and a deeper entrenchment in selfishness.

What needs to change, then, is our foundation. That should go without saying. But acknowledging that is not enough in and of itself. Being convinced that this change needs to happen is not enough in and of itself. Neither is commitment or will or tenacity. All of those things are still rooted in self.

What we need in order to move toward change is conviction.

POST SCRIPTS

PS to the Non-Church

This is the bare-bones, basement-level, stripped-back place where why we do what we do is clearly seen. For you, as you think about your own life, I'm sure there are motivations behind your actions that you are—at times—not proud of. That is to say, I'm sure you can resonate with the level of discomfort that accompanies this kind of exposure. It is the rare individual who truly enjoys having all of their flaws put out on the driveway for everyone to see.

The "whys" that become visible here at this level are the reasons that the church has failed you or harmed you. These are also the reasons that the church has failed Jesus and his Great Commission call.

I hope you can see at this level that these failings are not unique to the church but that they are shared amongst all people everywhere. This is a sort of tragic beauty about the church; that God has entrusted this work of love and grace to the very same people who are so often unloving and ungracious.

I hope you can see at this level that the failings of the church are the failings of the people in it and not of the Savior they struggle to follow.

PS to the Church

As you consider the unearthed landscape around you, what do you see? Don't shrink back at this point. The temptation is going to be great right now for you to just look around and, because there is significant work involved in moving forward, to just pack it in. Even if it is uncomfortable—especially if it is uncomfortable—don't give into the temptation to give up and go back to where you started. Don't lean on your crutch of defensiveness in the face of the accusations of obligated, entitled, lazy, and selfish—instead, take the hint and understand that your defensiveness is further accusing you. Your defensiveness is the same attitude that motivated the Pharisee to pray, thanking God that he was so much better—so much holier—than that awful, sinful tax collector.

A number of years ago I worked in a residential care facility. One of the kids in my care excelled in sports and football was his best sport. I picked him up after practice one day and he was really down on himself. After asking a few question I discovered that his coach had been really nitpicky on some of his mistakes that day. In an effort at empathy, I said, "Yeah, it can be hard when the people you trust aren't encouraging." He looked up at me at that point and said, "What do you mean? He *is* encouraging me—he's encouraging me to do better and he's showing me how."

Be encouraged as you face these deficiencies church. God has laid out for us exactly what our foundation should be. He is encouraging us to do better and he's showing us how.

8

Conviction

CONVICTION IS A BIG topic. It is far too big a topic to cover exhaustively in any book, much less in one chapter of a book. So, what follows will serve these two purposes: first, to provide a basic outline of the Holy Spirit's work of conviction and, second, to apply that to the work of unearthing the church.

HOLY SPIRIT

The Holy Spirit is sometimes referred to as the Spirit of God or the Spirit of Christ or just the Spirit (Rom 8:9–11). He is God at work in the hearts and minds of Christians. He—that is, the Holy Spirit—is the helper who Jesus promised to his disciples, the helper who would come when Jesus went to heaven (John 14:26). The Holy Spirit came on the day of Pentecost (Acts 2) and has been active in the lives of Christians and the church ever since.

There are various works or actions that Scripture attributes to the Holy Spirit. He gives believers spiritual gifts (1 Cor 12:4–11), he gives us direction (Acts 16:6–10), he convicts us of sin (John 16:7–11), and he guides us in the truth (John 14:25–26). Though there are many more things that the Scriptures outline as the work of the Holy Spirit, it is these last two—convicting of sin and guiding in truth—that will be our focus.

CONVICTION

Said very simply, conviction is becoming convinced that something is not how it should be. Getting a little more specific, conviction for the Christian is when the Holy Spirit shows you that something in your life is contrary to the will of God and that it must change.

In John 16, Jesus tells his disciples that when the Holy Spirit comes "he will convict the world concerning sin and righteousness and judgment: concerning sin, because they do not believe in me; concerning righteousness, because I go to the Father, and you will see me no longer; concerning judgment, because the ruler of this world is judged" (John 16:8–11).

Here is a simple way of thinking about the work of the Holy Spirit. Do you remember the first time you lied to your parents or to a teacher or any adult you respected? You know that feeling in your chest—that rapid heart beat—that you knew for sure was going to reveal your secret. You may have had clammy palms or a sweaty forehead. Maybe your breathing was a little stifled or you stumbled over your words. You had all of these physical symptoms of lying—these symptoms of being worried about being caught—as you opened your mouth to speak your untruth.

Why did you feel that way? Because you knew that what you were doing was wrong. Every fiber of your being was begging you to not do it, to not tell the lie. You knew, in a deep way—perhaps a spiritual way—that what you were doing was wrong and that you should, at once, do an about face and tell the truth.

Conviction, as brought on by the moving of the Holy Spirit, is all of that and more. Conviction comes upon us and makes us aware that, not only are we thinking or speaking or doing something that is wrong, we are thinking or speaking or doing something that contrary to the very will of God. Conviction for the Christian is the pairing of guilt over the wrong done with sorrow for having placed self over and above God. Conviction is when we see our lives on the backdrop of God and his perfect will and we are overcome with our sinfulness.

This is why this Scripture (John 16:8-11) speaks of sin and righteousness and judgment. It is because the conviction of the Holy Spirit is not simply a feeling of guilt or shame for having been found out. It is much more than that. The conviction of the Holy Spirit entails acknowledging our sin in the light of God's righteousness and knowing—knowing deep within our hearts—that we are deserving of judgment for all of our sin.

Conviction is the tool that God uses in order to move us toward him. If there was no conviction, no one would ever see reason to do other than they have always done. Similar to the way that social norms are upheld through expectation and disappointment, God moves our hearts toward him by graciously allowing us to engage with his expectations so that we can understand clearly when we have not met them.

I use the word "graciously" with this intent: if judgment—that is, God's determination of our eternal zip code—is on the line, then it is *gracious* that God allows us to see his expectations and for the Holy Spirit to place his conviction on our hearts so that we can see our error and turn to God.

It's important to remember through this discussion of conviction and the ways in which we are motivated to think and speak and act as a result of that conviction, that our eternity—whether it be connection to God or separation from him—is not determined by what we do. Instead, it is determined by whether we have faith in Jesus whose resurrection overcame the penalty for our sins. We do not act upon the conviction of the Holy Spirit in order to be saved; instead we act upon the conviction of the Holy Spirit because we've already been saved (Jas 2:14-18).

The Holy Spirit consistently works in the lives of believers to convict of sin, showing us the things in our lives that need to be changed or rejected—this is true for the individual and this is true for the church.

So, what convictions have come upon you as you have undergone this process of unearthing? What foundational elements of the way you live or the way your church functions have you considered and found to be selfish? What is the Holy Spirit convicting you to get rid of?

The answers to these questions are not the end of the matter. Identification of what needs to be purged is only useful to the degree that you purge them and then leave them purged.

Consider the garage that needed to be cleaned out. You labored to remove everything from the garage. You very carefully swept every inch of the floor, getting all of the sand and leaves and other debris off the floor and out the door. You evaluated all of the stuff that you took out of the garage, throwing away what was deemed useless and putting back in place what was deemed useful. You stepped back and evaluated the work and were satisfied, knowing that what you had done was good.

But, how many of us know that one person who sometimes has a hard time letting things go? How many of us *are* that person? You know, the person who, perhaps begrudgingly, agrees to throw away that box of old magazines. Maybe they even carried that box of magazines to the side of the road. But, when the sun goes down they slink back out to the roadside, rescue the box, and put it back in the garage in a place where it won't be discovered.

Do you have a hard time actually letting go?

Of course you do. We all do. The Scriptures outline this human tendency again and again. Jesus, warning his disciples not to fall into temptation, said, "The spirit is indeed willing, but the flesh is weak" (Matt 26:41). Paul addressed this when he wrote, "I do not understand my own actions, for I do not do what I want, but I do the very thing that is hate" (Rom 7:15). Or, to put it a little more graphically, Prov 26:11 says, "Like a dog returns to his vomit is a fool who repeats his folly."

Even as you submit to the work of the Holy Spirit, do not confuse your acknowledgment of what needs to change with the conviction to change. The conviction that comes by way of the work of the Spirit is an impulse that leads to action. When we are convicted, we are moved to repent of the thoughts, words, and actions that were out of line with God's will and we are moved to walk away from them forever.

What this means is that our submission to the work of the Holy Spirit only *begins* with conviction. If conviction is to take root and have an impact on our lives and on our churches, then we must also submit to the Holy Spirit's guidance. This brings us back once again to the Great Commission so let's put these pieces together.

In Matt 28:19-20 Jesus said, "Go therefore and make disciples of all nations, baptizing them in the name of the Father and of the Son and of the Holy Spirit, teaching them to observe all that I have commanded you." In John 14:26, Jesus said, "The Helper, the Holy Spirit, who the Father will send in my name, he will teach you all things and bring to your remembrance all that I have said to you." Then, In Acts 2, the Holy Spirit comes and begins doing the work that Jesus said the Holy Spirit would do as the disciples began boldly teaching the message of the gospel of Jesus.

When we encounter the Holy Spirit, we are convicted of the ways in which we fall short of God's righteousness. We are moved to repentance and to a new life in Jesus. That new life is marked by the continued work of the Holy Spirit as he guides us in our thoughts, words, and actions, empowering us to do the work of the Great Commission, and giving us the knowledge we need when we need it.

We cannot get to that place if we refuse to acknowledge the faults in our foundation. We cannot get to that place if we reject the words of Jesus. We cannot get to that place if we won't admit our selfishness. Encountering the Holy Spirit in this way—leading to conviction and repentance—highlights these truths and leads us to the next and last step in the unearthing process.

POST SCRIPTS

PS to the Non-Church

There have been many bits and pieces through this unearthing process that have been very churchy in terms of focus and lingo and yet, up until now, many of those things have had some amount of crossover appeal. That is to say, you've probably read through many of these chapters and the challenges contained therein and thought, "Sure, but that's not unique to people in the church. That's true for most everyone."

Most folks would likely be in agreement with the idea that what you do is a good indicator of what you believe. Most folks would also line up in favor of the idea that the ends do not justify the means. These are ideas that nest well within culture generally.

But here—though there may be non-church parallels to conviction like the human conscience or common sense—no non-church parallel really comes close to what is experienced in Holy Spirit conviction. This is a conviction that does not come in consultation with personal preference or social expectations. It does not come in consultation at all. Holy Spirit conviction is something that is imposed over and above what the Christian might otherwise feel, think, or believe and Christians, if genuinely convicted, ought to feel compelled to enact the conviction. To do otherwise is to sin.

I wanted to be clear about this implication for you as we move into the next couple of chapters ("Deny Self" and "Covenant") for two reasons: first, because without conviction there is no church and second, it is my contention that all of the harm that the church has caused has been because the church has failed to act on Holy Spirit conviction.

PS to the Church

I assume that you've been reading the postscripts for the non-church as well as the postscripts for the church, but just in case you haven't been, stop, go back, read the postscript for the non-church above, and then come back and pick up in the next sentence.

There are two bits in particular that I want you to consider:

1. All of the harm that the church has caused has been because the church failed to act on Holy Spirit conviction.
2. Christians, if genuinely convicted, ought to feel compelled to enact the conviction. To do otherwise is to sin.

Sin has come up a few times thus far—mostly in the context of the forgiveness that Jesus offers all who have faith in him—but it hasn't come up as an accusation. I want to acknowledge that there is an accusational tone at play here.

Church, please understand that refusal to be unearthed—refusal to submit to the conviction of the Holy Spirit and refusal to be obedient to the commands of Jesus—is sin. Any and every time we have done things according to preference or selfishness, we have asserted our will over the conviction of the Holy Spirit and we have harmed ourselves, our witness, Christ's church, and the people we've been called to serve.

Conviction is when the Holy Spirit shows you that something in your life is contrary to the will of God and demands that you change it.

What have you been shown? What must you now change?

9

Deny Self

IN THE STANDARD MARRIAGE vows that are exchanged between would-be wife and husband, you will often hear a line something like this: "I promise to love and comfort you, honor and keep you, and forsaking all others, I will be yours alone as long as we both shall live." It is a beautiful and necessary sentiment to state and to hold to as a man and woman enter the covenant of marriage. When the couple exchanges those words—forsaking all others—it is a promise not just to subordinate all other relationships to this relationship, it is also a promise to subordinate self in favor of spouse.

When a man and a woman get married, they are committing to set aside their individual preferences for the sake of the marriage and for any children who might result from their marriage. In this way, they are rejecting their former lifestyle which was marked by selfishness in favor of a lifestyle that is marked by self-denial.

"I choose," both man and woman declare, "to place you and us above me."

This is a beautiful reflection of the commands of love that Jesus highlights in Matt 22, Mark 12, and Luke 10. One of the religious leaders asked Jesus, "Which commandment is the most important of all?"

To this Jesus responded, "You shall love the Lord your God with all your heart and with all your soul and with all your mind and with all your strength. The second is this: You shall love your neighbor as yourself. There is no other commandment greater than these" (Mark 12:28–31).

The expectation that Jesus has for people who are in relationship with him is that we would use every ounce of our being to love him—heart, soul, mind, and strength. There is no aspect of who we are that is not expected to be committed and devoted to this way of life. Since this is the case, there is no room within the commands of God for us to withhold any part of who we are from him; from full and complete submission to God and his will. Even the way that we love ourselves and the way that we love others is in submission to God and his will.

This is a full and complete denial of self-determination and personal will. In other words, the prime attitude that is at the heart of love—whether in relationship with God, friend, or spouse—is selflessness. As the conviction of the Holy Spirit comes upon us, we are moved from thoughts, words, and actions that are aimed at pleasing ourselves and toward thoughts, words, and actions that are aimed at satisfying God's will.

Church, do not nod your head in agreement too quickly here, thinking about how this is so true and, "If only the culture could see this, we'd be in a much better place." Do not move so quickly past wrestling with the fruit of your church and what that reveals about your beliefs and actions. Do not move so quickly past the foundational elements of obligation and entitlement and laziness that have been unearthed. Don't settle once again into an attitude of finger-pointing.

Yes, the culture outside of the church does not know and understand and exhibit the love of God or the commands of Jesus—why should they?—but how well are we doing in that regard? A large part of the reason we undertake the process of unearthing the church is because of the harm that our mishandling of the love and grace and calling of Jesus has caused the people we would often rather accuse than befriend.

It is our sin and error and shortcoming, church, that needs to be addressed. The comparison in view right now is between us and God, not between us and the people God has sent us to serve.

What, then, is the standard that we are called to?

This standard comes into full view in the words of Jesus that are found in Matt 16:24-26. Leading up to these words, Jesus had taken time to explain to his disciples that he would go to Jerusalem and that he would suffer and would be killed and, when all of that was done, the he would be raised from the dead.

To the disciples this was a shock. Their vision of the life and ministry of Jesus and the results of that life and ministry was quite different from this image that Jesus laid out. What they had envisioned—along with most of the Jewish people of the time—was a Messiah who would come as a conquering king. What they wanted to see was Jesus take up a sword and go to Jerusalem to make the occupying Roman forces submit to him. Their desire was to see the kingdom of God come in power and glory through military conquest.

So, when Jesus told the disciples that he would go to Jerusalem only to be killed by the very people that they wanted to overthrow, it didn't matter what he had to say after that. It is as if they didn't even hear him say that he would be raised from the dead. Instead of engaging with the narrative that Jesus outlined, wondering about what it might mean, it says that "Peter took [Jesus] aside and began to rebuke him, saying, 'Far be it from you, Lord! This shall never happen to you'" (Matt 16:22).

As a kid I remember daydreaming about back-talking to my parents or to my teachers. I used to work out just exactly what I would say the next time they yelled at me. Then, when the opportunity came, I always swallowed the words for fear of what kind of trouble I would cause for myself.

And yet, here we see Peter rebuking Jesus. I can't even imagine.

Jesus' response was swift and stern. "Get behind me, Satan! You are a hindrance to me. For you are not setting your mind on the things of God, but on the things of man" (Matt 16:23).

Jesus counter-rebukes Peter, upping the ante by referring to him as Satan, telling him that his mind is set on the wrong things, and it is at this point that Jesus lays out the expectation—the standard that we are held to:

> If anyone would come after me, let him deny himself and take up his cross and follow me. For whoever would save his life will lose it, but whoever loses his life for my sake will find it. For what will it profit a man if he gains the whole world and forfeits his soul? Or what shall a man give in return for his soul? (Matt 16:24–26)

Don't miss the forcefulness of these words. Jesus is looking at his disciples and he is saying that the only way for them to be his followers is if they deny themselves. Pairing that with the love commands, we see that the only way to love God is that we would deny ourselves. Not just deny, though. The language that Jesus uses here is that of dying. When Jesus uses the cross imagery, he does so with the purpose of showing the disciples that they must be willing to die. It is only in dying for Jesus that they can actually find their lives.

From there, Jesus lays out a rhetorical question upon which the whole premise, process, and weight of unearthing the church hangs: "For what will it profit a man if he gains the whole world and forfeits his soul?"

The only reason the church would not completely and immediately lay itself bare before Jesus in the conviction of the Holy Spirit is if we have decided that what we have—our traditions, practices, entitlement, laziness, and selfishness—is more valuable than our souls and the souls of the people we're called to love, serve, evangelize, and disciple.

None of us would want to say that about ourselves, certainly, but is it a fair assessment?

Consider this story that has been told over and over.

It is the tale of a church with a long and storied past, spanning generations. In days, long past, the church was full to overflowing with families, young children, and hope for a long and prosperous future. Relying on their numbers and the strength of their families—and, truth be told, their fear of losing them—the church began focusing on meeting the needs of their members, caring primarily for those in the congregation, more so than for those in the community.

Over time, as families aged and children went off to college, the church found that they were shrinking significantly and quickly. So, they committed to outreach, not for the sake of saving souls but for the sake of saving their congregation. They were somewhat successful as they started, several families joining the ranks. But, as these new families began to express opinions that were contrary to the way the church had always done things, they were overlooked or mistreated and they eventually left.

The church, now on the verge of failing, began worrying about its money. They wanted to be sure they had enough to keep the doors open. So, they squirreled away a few hundred thousand dollars so they could stay open indefinitely. A number of years later, the congregation now having dwindled to a handful of bitter old saints, the church is forced to close its doors.

Most of you have likely heard that story a time or two. Some of you have even been one of those bitter old saints.

What did it profit that church?

Yes, rhetorical questions bear the weight of their own answers, but—just so that it is clear—when Jesus asks, "What will it profit a man if he gains the whole world and forfeits his soul?" the answer to that question is "nothing." The only profit, the only gain, the only benefit that anyone can ever receive comes through denial of self. The only profit, the only gain, the only benefit that the church can receive comes through denial of self.

In self-denial, the conviction of the Holy Spirit and the clearing of the temple grounds come together. Jesus speaks into our lives telling us clearly that we must deny ourselves—that there are things in our lives that we have been holding onto that are keeping us from being able to follow where he leads. The Holy Spirit comes to us, as promised by Jesus, to show to us exactly what those things are—convicting us of the things in our lives that are contrary to God's will—and then driving those things out of our lives.

In 1 Cor 6:19–20, Paul says, "Do you not know that your body is a temple of the Holy Spirit within you, whom you have from God? You are not your own, for you were bought with a price. So glorify God in your body."

It is a straightforward point of connection between what Jesus did when he entered the temple grounds and what he does when he enters our hearts. It is no less violent and no less forceful. Jesus tells us that we must deny ourselves, the Holy Spirit brings that conviction, and then he begins the work of driving out from within us everything that is keeping us from thinking, speaking, and acting in ways that honor and glorify God.

Jesus comes to us to drive things out of our lives. It is a forceful process that we need to welcome. When Jesus shows us things that are not in line with his word and his will, we need to submit to his word and his will. Denial of self, then, is far less about what you do than it is about what God does in you. It is a denial of selfishness and self-determination in favor of Christlikeness and submission to his will.

You cannot, however, embark on this journey by yourself. The journey of self-denial requires the conviction and the power of the Holy Spirit, but it also requires people to walk with you. Moving down to the foundation level on this unearthing process has largely consisted of considerations of church-wide attitudes and actions. Likewise, self-denial, though it is an intimate process that takes place in the heart of the individual at the moving of the Spirit, can only be nurtured within the church.

As in the generic story of the large church that failed because it was selfish, that church was comprised of many individuals with individual stories and convictions, successes and failures. When churches fail, it is a common practice for those who are participants in the failure to look for reasons, excuses, and people to lay fault on. No matter how many individuals were faithful followers of Jesus and how many refused to yield to his lordship, churches flourish together and churches fail together. Despite appearances to the contrary, no church flourishes or fails because of one individual. A flourishing church that falls into complete disarray over the failing of one individual was never really flourishing to begin with.

Similarly, no Christian can truly flourish as an individual. Denial of self, in this case, comes in the form of humility in the face of a life that was never intended to be undertaken in isolation. At creation, God declared that it is not good for people to be alone. Moses needed people to support him in leading the people of Israel. Paul needed people to support him in his travels. As I examine my own life, I do not have to think very long before I think of several people who have been instrumental in my growth and development. This relates to my walk as a Christian, my walk as husband and father, my walk as a pastor, and my walk as a chaplain. There is nothing of value that I have ever done in my life that was accomplished in isolation. This is certainly the case for you as well. Every Christian needs the support of like-minded people in order to be successful in their self-denial.

How do you expect to be able to deny yourself if you rely only on yourself?

POST SCRIPTS

PS to the Non-Church

Self-denial is in opposition of modern cultural ethics. "Follow your heart." "Live your dreams." "You do you." These ideas and ethics reveal a self-centeredness that the culture embraces and that the church is supposed to reject.

The times when the church causes harm are the times when the church adopts this modern cultural ethic. It is when the church has refused to deny self that the church has done the things that people rightly shame it for. You rightly have a higher expectation for the church; that it would behave differently than the culture, that it would act in love, and that it would hold itself to this higher expectation as well.

In this sense, the real complaint the culture has against the church is when the church reflects culture and not Christ.

Every relationship you have—whether with family, friends, coworkers, significant others, or anyone else—suffers when you are selfish. That's not news to you. What may be news to you, however, is the fact that the ways to make your relationships flourish—self-denial, considering others more highly than yourself, seeking the good of others—come from the mouth of Jesus and the word of God.

I want for the church to live up to this standard so that you can experience this kind of love. This, indeed, is the kind of love that Jesus offers you and commands the church to offer you as well.

PS to the Church

This is an action step. This is the "trash to the road" step. This is the step in which we actively engage the power and work of the Holy Spirit to show us and remove from us all of the stuff that we've laid out on the driveway that needs to be purged; all of the stuff that is harming us, our witness, and those we're called to serve. This is the step in which we, as individuals and as a church, speak with conviction the words of John the Baptist and say, "Christ must increase, but I must decrease" (John 3:30).

Back in chapter 3—"Modern Mission"—I recounted a time when I posted the following on Facebook: "Perhaps the best thing that could happen to the church in America is that all our buildings be demolished." Though I regret that that is how I felt back in 2016, what if it actually happened?

What if it became clear that the best path forward for *the* church—or just for *your* church—was a path that didn't include a building? What if it became clear that the path forward only allowed for lay leaders (that is, "nonprofessional" pastors/leaders)? What if the path forward was no websites, no socials, and no streaming? What if, in denying self, everything was stripped away and all you had left was the gospel of Jesus and his command to go? Would that be enough?

10

Covenant

THE CHURCH, BY GOD's design, is inherently relational. This is a reflection of God himself, eternally existing as Father and Son and Spirit. This is a reflection of the nature of humanity, that God created us to be in relationship with one another and to crave relationship with one another. This is a reflection of the nature of our relationship with God himself, the relationship that we broke through our selfish sinfulness and that he restored through the sacrifice of Jesus.

Humanity was created by a relational God to be in relationship with each other and with him. Every work of God since the time sin entered the universe has been geared toward restoring that relationship and bringing full glory back to himself. As such, the idea of relationship within the church is an extension of the perfection of God and his perfect image for humanity and for the church.

The importance of this is accentuated in those times when church relationships have been strained; times when there have been lingering disagreements or hurt feelings that the involved parties are unwilling to address. When these things come up, we are all involved parties because we are all impacted by the strained relationship.

Do you enjoy being in conflict with the people you care about? Do you enjoy having strained relationships with the people you are supposed be encouraging and loving and doing the work of the church with? The answer to each of those questions is "of course not," and yet are you more likely to live with conflict in the undercurrent of a relationship or in the church than you are to bring it up in conversation? The answer to that question is also "of course."

It is a baffling condition that we create for ourselves and, though we hate it so much, we often perpetuate it for ourselves.

In this post-COVID world, fewer and fewer people have relationships that they would describe as close. People feel alone and isolated in numbers far higher than ever before. Some social scientists attribute this to the pandemic and the lingering effects of social isolation. Other social scientists attribute it to a reality that's been in place for years that was only brought into sharp view by the social isolation the pandemic necessitated. Whichever analysis is correct, the impact remains: people are lonely and getting lonelier. A recent survey found that 49 percent of respondents had three or fewer people in their lives whom they would describe as "close friends." This survey also found that 12 percent had no close friends at all (American Perspectives Survey, May 2021).

This phenomenon is not to the exclusion of the church as this survey was done across political, religious, and socioeconomic lines. It doesn't matter what demographic or which intersection of demographics you consider, the population of the United State feels alone.

Taking these statistics to heart then, consider this: is it likely that one out of every two people you encounter has three or fewer close friends. Or, to make it a little more personal—not that that wasn't personal enough—fifty percent of the people reading this book is likely to be struggling with some measure of isolation or loneliness. These numbers are insufficient in painting a full picture of the state of friendship or loneliness in society, but it provides a helpful glimpse.

If that doesn't describe your situation, consider this a wake-up call to the reality of the lives of 49 percent of the people around you, whether in your home, your church, your work, or your community. If that description—isolated or alone—doesn't describe you, consider this a call to action and a challenge to look and see how you might become the connection someone is looking for, the connection that someone is in need of.

When holding that reality up in comparison to the statement from the beginning of this chapter—"The church, by God's design, is inherently relational"—what does it suggest about how the church is doing at meeting the designed purpose of the church? It suggests that the church is not living up to the designed purpose of the church very well. And, if that's the case, what does this suggest about the way in which we are supporting each other as we seek to deny self? Yeah, we're not doing very well there either.

At the end of chapter 9 I asked the following question: how do you expect to be able to deny yourself if you rely only on yourself? Looking at these statistics, another question rises to the surface: how can we expect anyone to be able to deny themselves if they don't have anyone else to turn to?

Going back to the relational nature of the church, it is designed that way by God because the things that he calls us to do as his followers cannot be accomplished if we are all on our own. Obviously, relationship requires more than one person, but so also does fellowship and discipleship and teaching. What sense does the Great Commission make if relationship is not assumed? If Jesus did not intend for us to be in relationship with him, with each other, and with those to whom we are sent, none of the commands contained in the Great Commission make any sense.

Relationship is necessary. If we are to grow in the grace and knowledge of Jesus, we need people to teach us and to disciple us and to challenge us and to have fellowship with us. But more than that, we need people who are committed to do those things with us no matter the circumstances. That kind of commitment is rare, but it is the kind of commitment that is intended and expected to exist between church members. This commitment is called covenant.

COVENANT

A covenant is an agreement between two or more people in the presence of God; an agreement in which each person involved is responsible to God and to each other for upholding. Each person involved is fully aware of the demands of the covenant and each agrees to be held accountable to every other person and to God if they fail in their end of the covenant. Similar to the implications of wedding vows, a covenant is a binding set of agreed upon conditions for a relationship.

Though the idea and practice of covenant is evident throughout the Scriptures—God's covenant with Noah and humanity following the flood, God's covenant with Abraham, the covenant Jesus establishes with believers—there is no scriptural mandate for church covenants. Church covenants exist, then, not to satisfy a biblical requirement but to identify how church members are expected to live in relationship with each other according to principles that are outlined in Scripture. There are many clauses or stipulations that are common to church covenants, each one aimed at clarifying what the covenanting parties will or won't do as well as the reasons for these actions or restrictions, each one rooted in Scripture.

Some of these clauses point to the scriptural principal of unity within the church. Some of these clauses point to the scriptural principal that the church will do all things to the glory of God. Some of these clauses point to living lives of temperance or generosity. Some speak about the necessity of raising children according to the instruction of the Lord.

Of all of the typical clauses a church covenant includes, there are two that highlight the necessity of covenant in the support of unearthing the church through the denial of self: the first is the clause that points to the importance of gathering with other believers on a regular basis and the second is the clause that points to the importance of carrying each other's burdens.

GATHERING

In Heb 10:24-25 we read this: "And let us consider how to stir up one another to love and good works, not neglecting to meet together, as is the habit of some, but encouraging one another, and all the more as you see the Day drawing near."

How can we encourage each other in self-denial and in the love of the Lord and in all other manner of good works if we are not committed to meeting regularly with each other? The regular gathering of the church members is designed, in part, to provide a support structure for all of the work of the church—both its whole and its individual participants.

Your relationships with people are stronger when you make time for those relationships and they are weaker when you don't make time. It is just that straightforward. Is there any reason to expect a different outcome for our relationships in the church? No. When we make a covenant with each other in the church, we are committing in part to meeting regularly.

CARRYING EACH OTHER'S BURDENS

The commitment to come together with the members of your church on regular basis strengthens relationships and sets the groundwork necessary for this typical covenantal clause. Galatians 6:2 tells us straightforwardly, "Bear one another's burdens, and so fulfill the law of Christ." Taking it a step further, Rom 12:15 challenges church members to "rejoice with those who rejoice, weep with those who weep."

As a hospital chaplain, I get multiple calls daily to go to the room of a person I've never met for the purpose of listening, empathizing, caring, and—at times—advising. Though each and every encounter is different because each and every person is different, there is a threshold effect that I always encounter. The threshold effect goes like this: before I am allowed access to a person's story or experiences, I have to demonstrate that I am trustworthy.

Though each patient's threshold is unique to them, each patient wants to vet me, my personality, my approachability, my sense of humor, my religious credentials, my work experience, my tastes in music or sports or politics—or some combination of these or many other categories—before they are willing to open up and share their story with me. This is a very reasonable—even sensible—exercise to undertake as it is important that we not just open up and share with anyone without first trying to make sure that person does not have ill intent.

A significant reason why it is necessary for church members to commit to regular gathering is that it is only in living out this commitment that we can be trusted to cross each other's thresholds. When we spend time together, we discover whether and with whom it is safe enough to share our stories and our struggles. We need to know that it is not going to backfire on us if we open up and share our burdens. We need to know that our sorrow is going to be met with empathy and that our joy is going to be met with celebration. We can only know this if we have spent ample time coming together and getting to know one another.

As was mentioned above, there are many other aspects of covenant that are important to the proper relational functioning of the church, but these two—gathering and carrying each other's burdens—are the two that make us more likely to be able to work together toward Great Commission goals. These two make the church far more likely to be a place in which we will find a connection that will serve to temper—or eliminate—our loneliness. These two—if the church lives them out well—make the church a place where people outside of the church are more likely to stick around long enough to find what they need.

A warning: don't confuse your comfort with the way that your church operates in these areas as evidence that your church is killing it covenantally. It is super easy—and super common—for people to be comfortable in the midst of dysfunction (that's the main reason we need to unearth the church). Don't let your constructively critical guard down.

Remember, church covenants do not exist to satisfy a biblical requirement; rather, they exist to identify how church members are expected to live in relationship with each other according to principles that are outlined in Scripture. Consider your church's covenantal aptitude—covenantal intelligence?—not in light of your comfort level but in light of the challenges of Heb 10:24–25.

Are you pushing each other toward love and good works?

Are you meeting together often and consistently?

Are you going out of your way to be encouraging?

Are you doing each of these things with increasing frequency and urgency?

If you said "no" to any of those questions, don't panic. What those "no" responses show you are opportunities to grow in covenant. Those questions offer a diagnostic that will give you greater clarity about what it is that God would have you do better or differently or more fervently. Doing covenant well will open up the doors to doing so many other things well. So don't panic or fret over these "no" responses; instead, thank God for showing these things to you and trust the Holy Spirit to lead you through them.

POST SCRIPTS

PS to the Non-Church

People in general have not been doing great relationally for a long time. These relational struggles used to be sort of hidden behind closed doors. People are historically pretty good at putting on a brave face and pretending everything's okay when everything is not okay.

I hope that you are okay; that you are not suffering in this pandemic of loneliness like so many are. But, if you're not okay—if you are lonely—I hope that you are able to find someone somewhere who can meet you in your loneliness. I further hope that that someone and that somewhere might be a Christian in a church.

This isn't an ulterior motive or a hidden agenda latent within the pages of this book. This is my hoped-for outcome, right out in the open. The church's selfishness has long prevented it from fully glorifying God in part because its selfishness has prevented it from being for you what Jesus commands it to be. I believe that the only solution to the separation and loneliness that is ravaging society is a relationship with God through Jesus *and* that the best place for that relationship to be nurtured is within the covenant community of the church.

I hope for the church to be unearthed so that it can become, once again, the place where you can find what God intends for you to experience—salvation and relationship.

PS to the Church

During the summer of 2020, after the pandemic had really set in and people were starting to understand that it was going to be a longer-lived thing than we had initially been told, I had a conversation with a close friend in my church. We were talking about COVID-19, how our church had responded, and what we hoped to do in the weeks and months to come.

At one point my friend took a thoughtful pause. After a moment or two he looked at me and he said, "I know they say we need to practice social distancing, but it seems like what we're doing is spiritually distancing."

Spiritual distancing.

That is the antithesis of covenant.

That is the root of an Americanized, individualized Christianity.

You simply cannot be the Christian you are intended to be if you are spiritually distanced from your church. You will not be nurtured, you will not be challenged, you will not be discipled, you will not have fellowship, and you will not grow in the grace and knowledge of our Lord Jesus Christ.

As you come out of the unearthing process, it is absolutely critical that you take covenant with your local congregation

seriously and that you encourage others to do the same. Rebuilding the church is only possible if you do so in submission to Jesus and in covenantal relationship within the church.
Repent from spiritual distancing.

11

Foundation Is Future

WE ARRIVE NOW AT the question that will determine where you go from here. Do you believe that the church—do you believe that *your* church—needs to be unearthed? Do you think that the current trajectory of your church is just fine and no alterations are necessary, or do you think that adjustments need to be made?

It is important to continuously come back to the personal—to come back to the real world situations that you are facing in your church and in your community. This is so important because this process can easily fall into the land of hypotheticals if you don't intentionally apply it to your personal experiences. When that happens—when you reduce it to hypotheticals—it becomes nothing more than an exercise in futility. It becomes just another "more talk less action" catharsis. Many of us can certainly imagine scenarios in which the critical evaluation set forth in this book would apply, but do you see the real world scenarios that you are actually facing and how these critical evaluations apply to those? Taking it out of the hypothetical and letting it resonate in the land of the real can be challenging, but it is also where the value lies.

My hope is that you do find this challenging; not because you have a hard time seeing how it connects to your experience of the church, but because you have a hard time seeing how it doesn't.

Foundation Is Future

In asking the question "do you believe your church needs to be unearthed?" the weight is not on whether your church needs to be unearth—it does—but on whether you can see it.

It is as true a statement as there can be to say that your church is imperfect. I'm so confident that this is true that I am willing to also assert that you will not disagree with that statement. No one who has considered the perfect love and will of God would dare make a statement to the contrary. To be human is to be in error and the church, itself comprised of error-ridden humans, is also in need of correction, reformation, and unearthing.

And yet—even though I know that no one would deny the imperfection of the church with a clear conscience—I also know that stasis is the preferred state of humanity. Stasis is the preferred state of our institutions. Of all the things humans hate doing, change is at or near the top of the list. People like to settle into patterns and routines that require little thought and the illusion of comfort. People become creatures of habit, choosing the same restaurants and the same grocery brands and the same vacation spots, so as to minimize the need to make new choices and decisions.

In some instances, these tendencies serve us well. There is great utility and value in choosing a place to live and a career to pursue. In fact, part of the purpose of covenant as laid out in the last chapter is to encourage this kind of commitment to the same group of believers over time.

The problem arises when the patterns, routines, and habits have shown themselves to be ineffective or harmful. In considering the outside-in perspective of the church, one of the things that we wrestled with was the ways in which the patterns and habits of the church can be aligned against the people the church is designed to minister to. Sometimes we discover that these patterns and habits are aligned against the influence of the Savior we are supposed to be serving.

In these situations, the human aversion to change is detrimental to everyone involved and everyone who might be impacted. The church should not be subject to these human tendencies, however, because the church is not a human institution. Yes, it is

Unearth the Church

comprised of human members, but it is covenanted together in the presence of God to be in submission to the headship of Jesus.

Newton's first law of motion, as I remember being taught in high school physics, goes like this: objects in motion resist changes in their motion unless they are acted upon by an external force.[1] Not being a physicist, I won't go any deeper in trying to explain the reasons why this is true. However, this is something that we can easily observe. If you throw a ball, the ball will eventually land on the ground because it's motion is being acted on by gravity. Or, if you throw the same ball toward someone holding a bat and that person swings their bat, hitting the ball, the ball will change direction because of the outside force applied by the bat.

Like it or not, for many churches Jesus is an outside force. Many of our churches have settled into a trajectory because of habit or comfort and they no longer understand why they do what they do. They no longer understand how or if what they're doing has a positive impact on themselves or on their spheres of influence. Some of these churches, when confronted with their feebleness, prefer to languish in their feebleness as opposed to allowing Jesus to act upon them.

In answering the question "do you think your church needs to be unearthed?" you are making a determination about your trajectory and your foundation. If you answer "yes, my church needs to be unearthed," you are acknowledging that there are elements of your church life that are not in line with God's perfect will and you would like for the Holy Spirit to act upon those things, bringing change and alignment. If you answer, "No, my church does not need to be unearthed," you are claiming that everything's fine in your church, that you've already arrived at God's perfect will or—worse—that you know you haven't come into alignment with the call of Jesus and the will of God, and that you're okay with that.

Both answers—affirmative or negative—ultimately make the same admission. Whether you answer "yes" or "no" you are admitting that your foundation is not what it should be. The difference

---

1. Hall, "Newton's Laws of Motion."

between the answers is seen not in what is admitted, but rather in what is preferred and where your church is headed.

To say "yes, my church needs to be unearthed" is to look at Jesus and to say, "We want to follow you more closely. We want you to be our full foundation." To say "no," on the other hand, is to look at Jesus and to say, "We think we're close enough."

"Yes" is the pursuit of Jesus. "Yes" is choosing Jesus as the foundation.

"No" is the rejection of Jesus. "No" is choosing self as foundation.

FOUNDATION IS FUTURE

This is the hinge-point for the entire project of unearthing the church. This is what determines if you will welcome the conviction of the Holy Spirit, denying self, moving toward the future that God has in store for his faithful followers or not.

To say that foundation is future is to say that you cannot build something other than what your foundation demands. This is not a proposition to be considered but a reality to be accepted. What you build on determines what you will build, it determines what type of structure can be sustained.

No church has ever set themselves to the task of constructing an organization and a ministry with the hope that it would fail. No. Every church that has ever existed has come into existence with the hope that it would be long-lived and fruitful. This is the mindset that nurtured the establishment of your church and every church in your town; yet, even though every church sets out to be successful in ministry, not every church does so from the same foundation.

There is only one foundation that can bear the weight of that kind of success. There is only one foundation that can bear the weight of pain and heartache. There is only one foundation that can bear the weight of sinners desperately in need of grace. There is only one foundation that can bear the weight of hope when all seems hopeless.

If you are still confused as to which foundation your church is built upon, consider again how your church contends with pain and heartache. How does your church do with welcoming sinners and offering grace? How does your church do in the face of tragic accidents or intentional harm? Does your church quickly turn inward, seeking to protect itself? Does your church often take prayer requests and turn them into gossip? Is your church committed to participation in weekly, monthly, and yearly events? Is your church just as enthusiastic about service projects as they are about the next summer picnic or the next fall festival?

There is only one foundation that can sustain a church in all of these things, producing within each member individually and within the church as a whole the good fruit associated with right belief and right action.

Consider that nagging thought that is tugging at the deep recesses of your mind right now. Consider that thought that is bubbling to the surface, the thought that is pointing at that one thing—or those five things—in your church that reveal a faulty, selfish foundation. That is the Holy Spirit working conviction in your heart and mind.

No one wants to admit when there is error or sin or faulty foundations in place in their lives or in their churches. No one wants to have to face that reality because it requires digging and unearthing and wrestling with conviction and making changes. But, no one who *doesn't* do those things will ever find themselves standing on the only foundation that gives hope for the future.

12

Next Steps

We desire each one of you to show the same earnestness to have the full assurance of hope until the end, so that you may not be sluggish, but imitators of those who through faith and patience inherit the promises.

—HEBREWS 6:11–12

WHAT IS YOUR DESIRE for the future of your church? What is your level of commitment to doing the work necessary to bring that desire into reality? Whose example will you follow as you persist in your faith, patiently enduring the hardships that will come your way?

In thinking about the next steps for the unearthed church, these are some of the questions that you need to wrestle with. While it is wonderful and necessary to have a vision for the future, that vision ultimately means very little if it is not paired with a plan for moving toward it and achieving it.

It is important to remember that no amount of prayer or study or conviction will have any impact on your life or on your church if it is not paired with the actions that the Holy Spirit prompts in conjunction with your prayer, study, and conviction. This is not to say that prayer, study, and conviction are useless; rather, that each of those things ought to propel you into Great Commission action. Your church will have no impact if it fails to act according to the conviction of the Spirit.

How, then, will you and your church endure until the end? Here I will offer four large targets to aim for—four things that will help you and your church stave off the inevitable temptation to retreat to the familiar, comfortable, and selfish church that we must leave behind. These four targets are (1) focus on what is good, (2) stay energized, (3) consider the next generation, and (4) practice discipleship.

FOCUS ON WHAT IS GOOD—PHILIPPIANS 4:8-9

These verses are as countercultural as they come. I do not mean countercultural in a church-versus-the-world sense; rather, I mean countercultural in an unearthed-church-versus-the-church sense. Churches that complain and constantly belittle and rail against the sinfulness of modern society and treat prayer requests as opportunities to gossip are churches that are indistinguishable from or worse than the very culture they complain about. Whereas these verses challenge Christians to focus on what is good, the church that refuses to be unearthed refuses to focus on what is good.

Why focusing on what is good is so important is because it draws our eyes and ears toward our Savior. By thinking about the things of God, we are in direct contact with his word and his will. Verse 9 tells us that when we practice all of the things that we have learned as followers of Jesus, "the God of peace will be with" us. This is a promise that meets us every step along the way. If what we are doing is good and it glorifies God, God will be with us in it.

STAY ENERGIZED—GALATIANS 6:9-10

These verses challenge the church to "not grow weary of doing good" and, as we do what is good, "let us do good to everyone."

This combination of challenges lays a heavy, but manageable burden on the church. Sometimes church members become demotivated in their work because they are not sure what their mission is, not sure what they should be doing next. These challenges to the church take away that uncertainty and, by extension, fight against the onset of demotivation.

There is a fatigue that settles in at times when you don't know what to do next. This fatigue may be due to the uncertainty mentioned above, it may be due to too many options, or it may be due to other personal or spiritual considerations. What this vague but definitive challenge—do not grow weary in doing good—does for those stuck in this place of fatigue is it multiplies the options. No longer are you concerned with figuring out which thing is the right thing to do next; your goal is now more about doing what is good, whatever that may be. Any of the good, God-glorifying options that lay before you are worth undertaking.

Staying energized as a next step, then, is possible because we are empowered by the Spirit to do good works and there are so many good works in front of us that we never need to worry about feeling useless or like there's nothing for us to do. This is good news for those who have left the church because they felt useless or like there was nothing for them to do. A church that understands and teaches that there is no end to the good work that we can do for the kingdom of God is a church that will be attractive to and embraced by the next generation.

CONSIDER THE NEXT GENERATION—EPHESIANS 6:4

One of the greatest disconnects that the church has endured in recent history is the disconnect between what we'll call "this generation" and "the next generation." As some from the next generation have walked away from the church, though there is a large catalog of reasons for their departure, one of the common reasons is that they did not feel as though they were contributing.

This is not a petty or immature complaint. People need to feel useful in order to feel connected. This is true of you no matter how old you are, no matter your religious affiliation, and no matter you age, ethnicity, or career. Everyone not only wants to feel useful, everyone needs to be useful.

There are many reasons why this issue is so persistent and so common among the next generation, and has largely always been common among every generation that was at one time considered the next generation (your parents experienced it, you experienced it, your kids experienced it, and so on). We'll focus here on two of the reasons this persists.

The first reason is distrust. It is a kind of ugly word and it is certainly not something we'd want to admit, but the truth is that we have a hard time trusting people who are younger than we are with much of anything. Why, the thinking goes, would I trust someone with less experience and less wisdom and less know-how with a job that I can do better and more efficiently myself?

This distrust bleeds over into the next generation and manifests itself as insecurity, unworthiness, and disconnection. The church's failure to give the next generation opportunities to try—even if they fail—communicates to them that they just aren't good enough. This distrust turns into a chasm between generations within the church and, when a group feels distrusted and unvalued, it is only a matter of time before they look for somewhere else where they might be useful.

The second reason the next generation often feels undervalued or useless is the "not my kids" syndrome. Each generation wants the next generation to have it better than they had it; they want to maximize happiness and minimize struggle. This is a very American phenomenon that is often very visible in parent-child relationships.

It goes like this: a child grows up in poverty, watching their parents work their fingers to the bone to provide, but never being able to get ahead. When that child grows up they promise themselves that their kids will never have to struggle like that. So, they set out to fulfill that promise and are largely successful. Their kids have everything they never had growing up. Their kids never want for anything and never have to strive for anything.

The "not my kids" syndrome often produces children who are unaccustomed to work, children who feel entitled, and children who are ignorant of what it takes in order to be successful. By raising their children in this way, the parent who only wanted their kids to have a better childhood than they had have robbed their children of the life lessons necessary to grow and thrive.

Applying this principle to the church yields the same result. When we shield the next generation from the struggles that go along with maintaining church health and being faithful in mission, we also shield them from the experiences that equip them to eventually take on those struggles themselves.

The work that we do now, we do not do so that the next generation does not have to do it; instead, we do it so that the next generation can learn how it is done.

Ephesians 6:4 challenges parents to "bring [children] up in the discipline and instruction of the Lord." Those nouns—discipline and instruction—are heavy words for children, but they are not too heavy for children. If the discipline and instruction of the Lord are good and necessary for our generation, they are good and necessary for every generation.

PRACTICE DISCIPLESHIP - EPHESIANS 4:22-24

It just makes sense that since Jesus has commanded the church to make disciples that the church ought to focus on making disciples. Discipleship is largely—if not entirely—about duplication. Not stamping *out* personality or individuality, but stamping each person or individual *with* the heart and mind of Christ. This is something that the church must do in house before it can have any credibility in its attempts to do it anywhere else. If people in the church do not resemble Jesus in the way that they think, speak, and act—if they are not pursuing Christlikeness—then any disciple-making venture they undertake outside the church is a fraud: you cannot make a disciple if you are not a disciple.

So, church, you must practice discipleship in your homes and in your congregations. You must start with your children and continue with your adults. Since you "are to grow up in every way into him who is the head, into Christ," you must make teaching and practicing Christlikeness the central feature of your church life (Eph 4:14).

According to this passage from Ephesians, this discipline and instruction will lead you to put off your old self, to be renewed in the spirit of your minds, to put on the new self, and nurture you in the likeness of God—in God's righteousness and holiness (Eph 4:22–24). You do not need to be perfected in righteousness and holiness in order to be effective in discipleship, but you do need to be in pursuit of righteousness and holiness.

When you do this well, you will be more equipped for the work of the Great Commission. When you do this well, you will be more effective in the work of the Great Commission. When you do this well, you will be the kind of church and the kind of people that those outside the church need you to be. When you do this well, things will change in your homes, your churches, and your communities. Indeed, without this fervent focus on discipleship, your church has no hope of being who Christ has called you to be, no hope of being the church the people in your community desperately need to you to be.

If you and your church are aiming at these four targets—focus on what is good, stay energized, consider the next generation, and practice discipleship—you will be aware of the ongoing work of God and the ways in which God is working through you. If you and your church are aiming at these four targets, you will be guarded against the temptation to, once again, opt for the foundation of selfishness. If you and your church are aiming at these four targets, it will serve as evidence that your church has been unearthed.

13

Unearthed Church

Unless the LORD builds the house, those who build it labor in vain. Unless the LORD watches over the city, the watchman stays awake in vain. It is in vain that you rise up early and go late to rest, eating the bread of anxious toil; for he gives to his beloved sleep.

—PSALMS 127:1-2

WHAT ABOUT THE FUTURE then? Since our foundation determines our future and since the only foundation that offers a hopeful future is Jesus, what is the future for this unearthed church? It would make no sense, after having gone through the unearthing process, for us to simply rebuild the church in whatever way we see fit. No, we undergo this process so that we are prepared for Jesus to rebuild us in his image.

What does the rebuilt, Christ-founded, and Christ-directed image of the church consist of? What does the unearthed church—the church that stands with Jesus as its foundation, cornerstone, and architect—look like?

The unearthed church is marked by five traits that make it sustainable and help to ensure its long-term viability. Each of these traits are things that were present in the early church, things that were apparent in the lives of Godly people throughout history, and things that were both taught and modeled for the church by Jesus and the apostles. These traits are prayerfulness, repentance, selflessness, empathy, and action.

THE UNEARTHED CHURCH IS PRAYERFUL

Whether you look at the life and teachings of Jesus or at the exhortations of the apostles or the examples of David and Daniel, what is clear is that prayer is central. Jesus' entire ministry was marked by prayer—both private and public—as he sought strength, connection, and guidance in the midst of his ministry. Paul regularly encouraged churches and fellow ministers of the gospel to pray, telling everyone to be in prayer for everyone else at all times. David turned to God in prayer throughout his lifetime as he wrote psalms of praise and sadness and fear. Daniel's devotion to God in prayer was so rock-solid that he still prayed to God even under penalty of death.

The unearthed church is committed to prayerfulness in all of these ways. The unearthed church understands that the denial of self and the conviction of the Spirit can only be accomplished and sustained in covenantal relationship—relationship with each other as well as with God. That relationship is nurtured best through regular fellowship and regular prayer.

The result of this devotion to prayer, though, accomplishes much more than the sustenance of relationships. It is also through regular prayer that the church and each individual member of it is convicted of sin and good works. The unearthed church understands that prayer nurtures every aspect of the life of the church and that the church would cease to be the church if it ceased to pray. Prayer is the first layer laid on the foundation of Jesus.

THE UNEARTHED CHURCH IS REPENTANT

To be clear here, repentance is marked by acknowledging a wrong thought, word, or deed and committing to turning away from that thought, word, or deed with the goal of never repeating it. Repentance is marked by sorrow over having chosen a selfish thought, word, or deed over and above a God-willed thought, word, or deed. This sorrow is brought on by conviction, the conviction that comes only through the work of the Holy Spirit. Repentance, then, should not be seen as an act of the will but as a submission of the will.

To say that the unearthed church is repentant means that members of the church are individually and collectively convicted of their sinfulness and have submitted themselves to the leadership of Jesus. This is a full about-face.

Repentance is not a momentary posture. Instead, repentance is a constant posture of the unearthed church; through regular prayer and submission to the will of God and the ongoing convicting and empowering work of the Holy Spirit, this church stands ready at all times to let go of any thoughts, words, or actions that are not—or are no longer—beneficial.

It is worth noting that the absence of repentance in a church is a clear and present sign that said church is fully entrenched in and founded on selfishness.

Conversely, the unearthed church has come to grips with its selfishness and the harms that selfishness has caused and has trusted the Holy Spirit to lead it away from that faulty foundation, placing it on the foundation of Jesus.

THE UNEARTHED CHURCH IS SELFLESS

This is the ongoing, ever-expanding result of self-denial. The unearthed church is inhabited by people who want to glorify God and serve him by caring for people and they accomplish this by reflecting the life and work of Jesus.

This idea is captured beautifully in the words of Paul as he wrote to the church in Philippi: "Do nothing from selfish ambition or conceit, but in humility count others more significant than yourselves. Let each of you look not only to his own interests, but also to the interests of others" (Phil 2:3-4).

This instruction is taken to heart by members of the unearthed church as they work to love and encourage everyone they encounter, both inside and outside of the church. Having a mindset of submission to Jesus—and an understanding of the way that Jesus came to serve and not to be served (Matt 20:28)—motivates them to serve people where they are, meeting their physical, spiritual, and emotional needs.

Jesus holds himself up as the example of this way of living, going so far as to say that this is the way that his followers *must* be. Just before making the statement that "the Son of Man came not to be served but to serve," Jesus told his disciples that the expectation for them—and for the unearthed church by extension—is that they would not be like the selfish leaders of the day. "It shall not be so among you. But whoever would be great among you must be your servant, and whoever would be first among you must be your slave" (Matt 20:26-27).

THE UNEARTHED CHURCH IS EMPATHETIC

Having empathy is a logical and necessary extension of being selfless. The unearthed church understands that to be selfless is to look beyond one's self. This is seen, in part, in the Philippians passage above—look to the interest of others—but empathy takes it a step further, going from simply looking out for the good of others to entering into the emotional experiences of others.

This is not sympathy. Sympathy is more in line with pity or the practice of feeling sorrow or sadness *for* someone's circumstances; it is the imposition of *your* emotional response onto someone else's experience. Empathy, on the other hand, is the participation with someone in their *own* emotional experience.

When it comes to sorrow, then, sympathy is sorrow *for* while empathy is sorrow *with*.

We see this expectation spelled out directly in Rom 12. Paul is outlining some characteristics of the true Christian—genuine love, zeal, patience, service, and joy to name a few—and, shifting his attention to the expected fruit of these characteristics, he has this to say about empathy: "Rejoice with those who rejoice, weep with those who weep" (Rom 12:15). Or, consider 1 Cor 12:26 where Paul says, "If one member suffers, all suffer together; if one member is honored, all rejoice together."

There are many times and many places in which preaching the gospel is exactly what needs to be done. There are times when what is good is to declare God's goodness and holiness and justice and grace. But there are also times when what we need to do is demonstrate God's goodness and holiness and justice and grace by simply entering into the sorrow or joy of the people we've been sent to serve. This is a true reflection of the ministry and life of Jesus who willingly put his Godly privileges aside so that he could enter into our lives as a man who comes alongside and as the God who saves.

THE UNEARTHED CHURCH IS ACTIVE

Each of these characteristics of the unearthed church thus far—prayerful, repentant, selfless, and empathetic—have this final characteristic in common; being active. This church prays and repents and lays selfishness aside and seeks to understand the experiences of other. This church takes action.

Remember the challenge of Jas 1:22: "Be doers of the word, and not hearers only, deceiving yourself." This verse makes the point that anyone who claims to be Christian while failing to act in accordance with the teachings of Jesus is deceiving themselves. The word of God, when it is implanted in the hearts and minds of a believer, demands that we take action. This aligns perfectly with the life and ministry of Jesus and it is in mirroring this aspect of the ministry of Jesus that we are most effective and most useful.

"We are to grow up in every way into him who is the head, into Christ, from whom the whole body, joined and held together by every joint with which it is equipped, when each part is working properly, makes the body grow so that it builds itself up in love" (Eph 4:15–16). Each member of the unearthed church has been equipped by the Holy Spirit to participate in the work of the church. The church is working properly when each member is working properly. Said a bit more succinctly, the church works when the members work.

These five traits all need to be present in the life of the unearthed church. While each on its own is important, their effect on the life of the church is multiplicative, not simply additive. These traits don't just pile on top of each other; rather, they interact in a way that has an impact far greater than the sum of the individual pieces. These traits work together, each one amplifying the other four.

It is in the conjunction of these five traits—prayerfulness, repentance, selflessness, empathy, and action—that the church best reflects the image that Jesus has for his church and that the church is most effective in accomplishing the work that Jesus has laid out.

Overlay these traits on the work that the Great Commission entails and it becomes clearer how necessary they are. A prayerful church that is committed to the Great Commission will be far more attuned to the working of the Holy Spirit. A repentant church that is committed to the Great Commission will be far more likely to rely on the power and will of God as it ventures out. A selfless church that is committed to the Great Commission will be far more concerned with the advancement of the kingdom. An empathetic church that is committed to the Great Commission will be better equipped to meet people where they are, loving them as they wrestle with the teachings of Jesus. An active church that is committed to the Great Commission will engage in the work necessary to accomplish the mission, having a willingness to undertake even the most difficult tasks.

Taking all of these outcomes together paints a picture of a church that is an imposing force. This is a desirable outcome.

At the end of chapter 4 I stated that the work of unearthing the church that relates to the outside-in perspective looks like this: listening to those who have been harmed, seeking to understand their perspective, considering their stories against the backdrop of the church that Jesus established, and in the instances the hurt has been caused because the church has failed to live up to that image, the church must repent and seek to set things right.

In every case, the hurt that the church has caused has not been because the church has been too bold in its Christlikeness but because the church has been too timid. The harm that the church has caused throughout history has always been due to too little commitment to Jesus and too much commitment to self. If the church's desire is to love people and lead them to Jesus, the church's only option is to be bold about its commitment to Jesus and his teachings.

For too long, the church has shied away from being imposing, seeking instead to blend into the background. The church has often preferred to take up as little space as possible in the community and in people's lives, sometimes apologizing for what little space it does inhabit. The church, divorced from the above traits, has stopped venturing into the world in a way that demonstrates a devotion to the Great Commission. This church has opted for careful and unchallenging messaging and ministry instead. This timid church—a church that is disconnected from its foundation and its calling—is a church that is worse than ineffective; this church is harmful.

Not so for the unearthed church. This church is founded on Christ, convicted by the Spirit, denies its preferences, and is committed to its relationship with each other and with Jesus. This church is characterized by prayer, repentance, selflessness, empathy, and action. The unearthed church takes up space in its community and in people's lives, obeying the Great Commission out of love for Jesus and for all who might come to know him.

The unearthed church understands just how necessary it was for Jesus to clear out the temple and then stands beside Jesus as he heals the blind and the lame. The unearthed church comforts people in their pain, loves people when no one else will, tends to the needs that religious people ignore, and pursues Jesus instead of growth.

Bibliography

Earls, Aaron. "Churchgoers Split on Existence of More Sexual Abuse by Pastors." Lifeway, May 21, 2019. research.lifeway.com/2019/05/21/churchgoers-split-on-existence-of-more-sexual-abuse-by-pastors/ https://research.lifeway.com/2019/05/21/churchgoers-split-on-existence-of-more-sexual-abuse-by-pastors.

Hall, Nancy, ed. "Newton's Laws of Motion." NASA, Aug 7, 2023. www1.grc.nasa.gov/beginners-guide-to-aeronautics/newtons-laws-of-motion.

"A New Chapter in Millennial Church Attendance." Barna, Aug 4, 2022. https://www.barna.com/research/church-attendance-2022.

Nieuwhof, Carey. "What Non-Christian People Really Think about the Church." Carey Nieuwhof, Jul 27, 2021. careynieuwhof.com/the-self-awareness-gap-what-non-christian-people-really-think-about-the-church.

Robinson, Phil Alden, dir. *Field of Dreams*. Written by Phil Alden Robinson. Universal Pictures, 1989.

Thumma, Scott. *Twenty Years of Congregational Change: The 2020 Faith Communities Today Overview*. Hartford, CT: Faith Communities Today, 2021. faithcommunitiestoday.org/wp-content/uploads/2021/10/Faith-Communities-Today-2020-Summary-Report.pdf.

Bibliography

www.ingramcontent.com/pod-product-compliance
Lightning Source LLC
Chambersburg PA
CBHW071450160426
43195CB00013B/2072